DICK MILLER

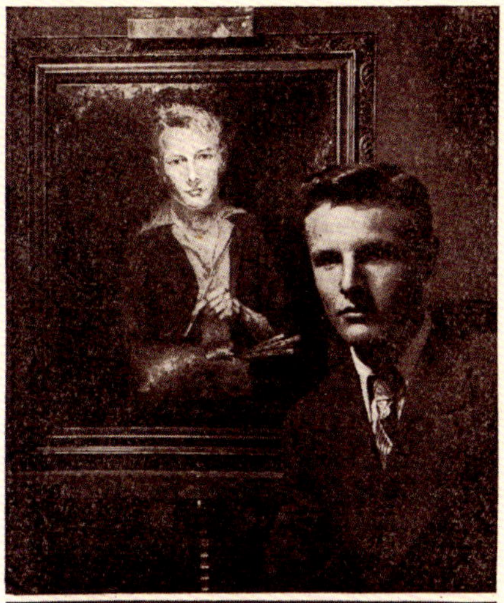

Self-portrait

EXHIBITION OF OIL PAINTINGS

FEBRUARY 16, TO MARCH 15, 1947

FAIRMONT STATE COLLEGE

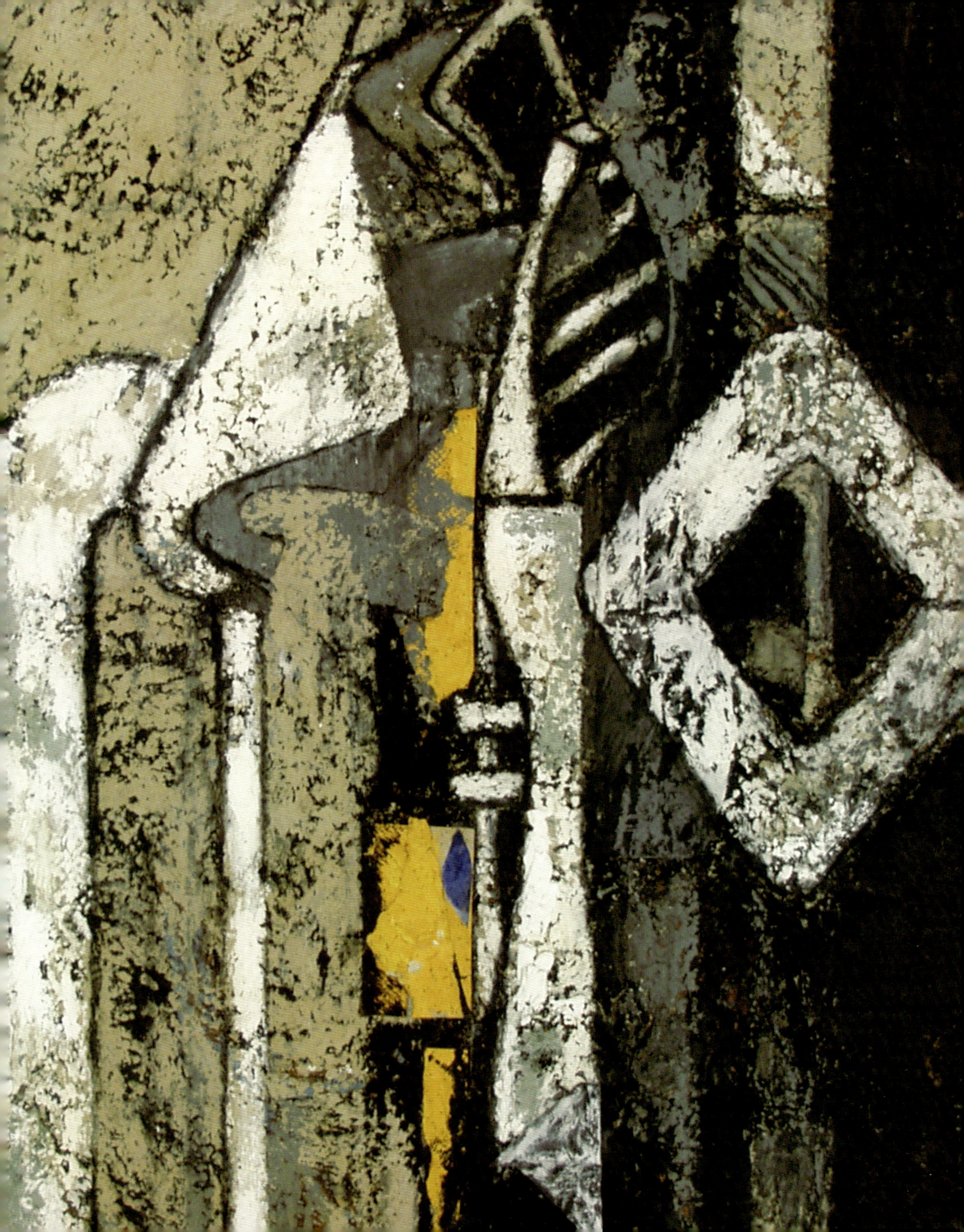

Richard Kidwell Miller

John A. Cuthbert
Curator

West Virginia Historical Art Collection
West Virginia University Libraries

This volume is published in conjunction with the exhibition Richard Kidwell Miller, West Virginia Historical Art Collection, West Virginia University Libraries.

Partial funding for this exhibition was provided by the National Society of Arts and Letters, Washington Chapter; James M. and Elizabeth H. Guiher; William Maxwell Davis, and Georgiana Morrison.

ISBN 0-9752925-0-1

Frontispiece: Yellow Jack II *(detail). Oil, oil stick and collage on canvas, 1990. West Virginia Historical Art Collection.*

Contents

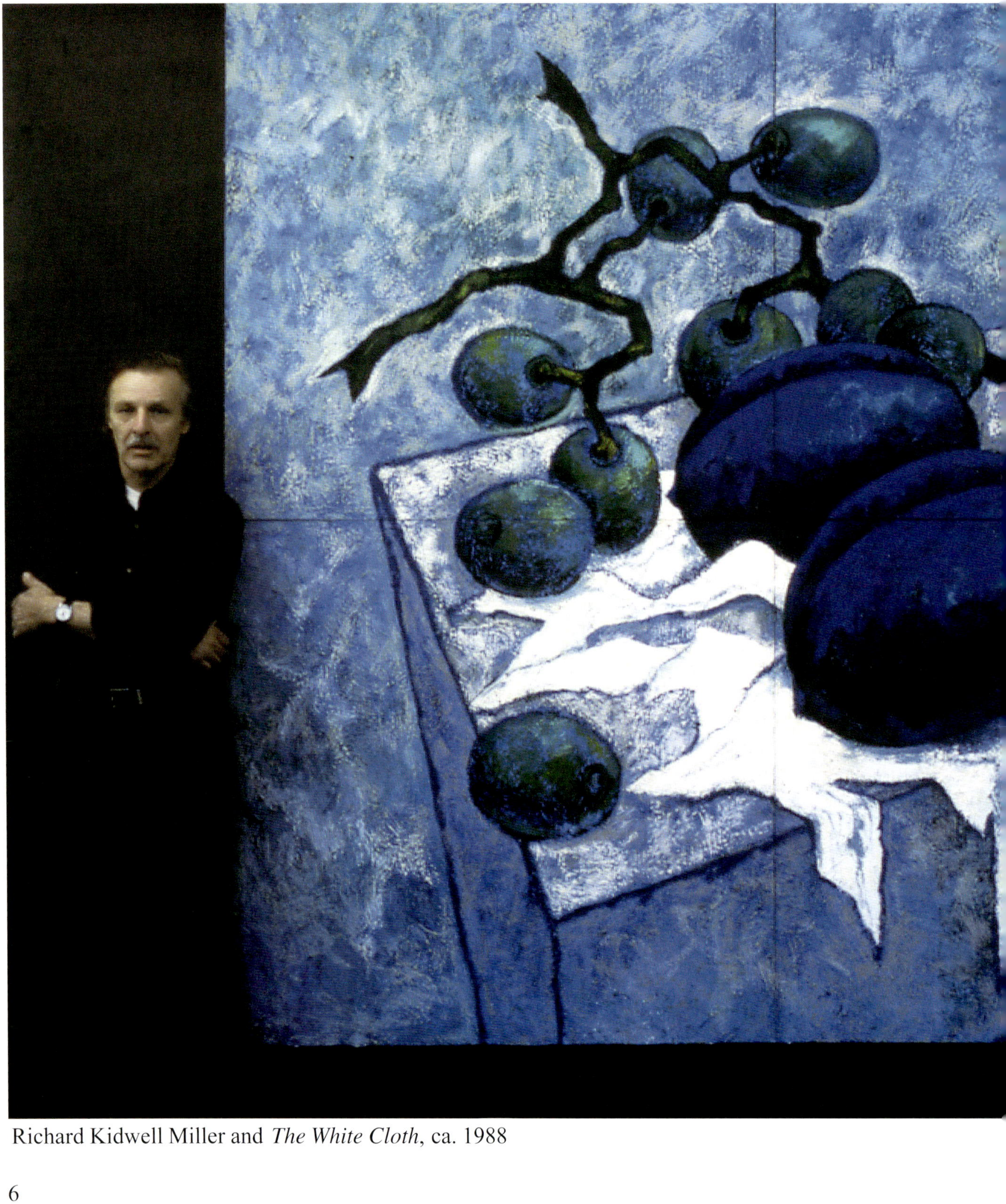

Richard Kidwell Miller and *The White Cloth*, ca. 1988

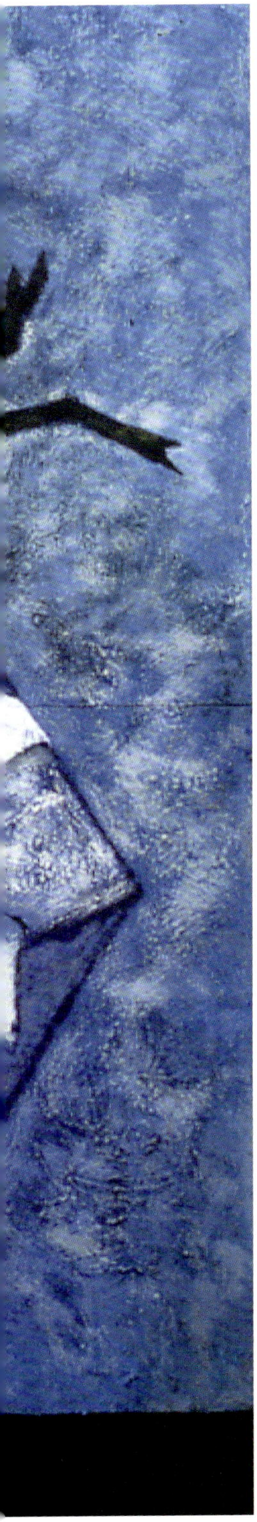

Foreword

Richard Miller's paintings are abstract, boldly yet sensuously painted, and iconic in effect. They pack a powerful punch but are also sensitively designed. Every element interacts precisely and "inevitably" with every other element to produce a tightly-knit whole. The result is work that is rock-solid in form and profoundly moving in substance and mood.

Miller has no formula for making art. If he can predict the outcome, he has to start over again. As he says, "I have to go beyond what I know."

And he does, as the evolution of his work proves. Thanks to his refusal to repeat himself and his insistence that he always move forward no matter what the risk, his paintings have gradually acquired ever-greater and more total formal and expressive clout.

They have become more compact and provocative. Black, red and a variety of browns and grays predominate, with white helping to create dramatic contrasts and occasional areas of blue serving to round off the color range. The overall effect is blunt and bold. This is tough, uncompromising art that makes its point simply and directly and without pulling its punches.

Miller may not be able to predict with precision how his paintings will look when they are finished, but he is absolutely clear about the effect he wants them to have.

Miller handles paint as judiciously and lovingly as a French chef handles food. And with the same balance of openness and control. In order to "go beyond" what he knows, he must be receptive to whatever the painting process itself brings up, and then incorporate it into the composition should it appear promising and in line with his overall intentions.

This openness to the unexpected enriches his art, for it often provides just the touch of color, texture or suggestive detail needed to solve or highlight a difficult passage. That is why he cannot be certain how his paintings will turn out. He may be in control, but the paint also has a say. How it is applied and shaped in accordance with his creative vision, and how it then complies or asserts itself in response, is crucial in determining the nature of his work and in giving it substance and meaning.

More than most painters, Miller enters into intense creative "dialogue" with everything that appears in his work. Nothing is inviolate. Everything is subject to alteration, removal – even to finding itself the center of attention. Shapes, colors, textures, linear patterns, bits of collage, everything and anything, become part of the mix before it slowly finds its rightful place in the composition.

Most of the time, everything comes together like clockwork to form a powerful and exquisitely designed work of art. At his best, Miller is a first-rate painter, but even when he falls a little short, and it seldom happens, what he produces is worthy of respect.

Simply put, Richard Miller is one of the best artists around. He has style and guts, and he has something to say.

Theodore F. Wolff
New York City

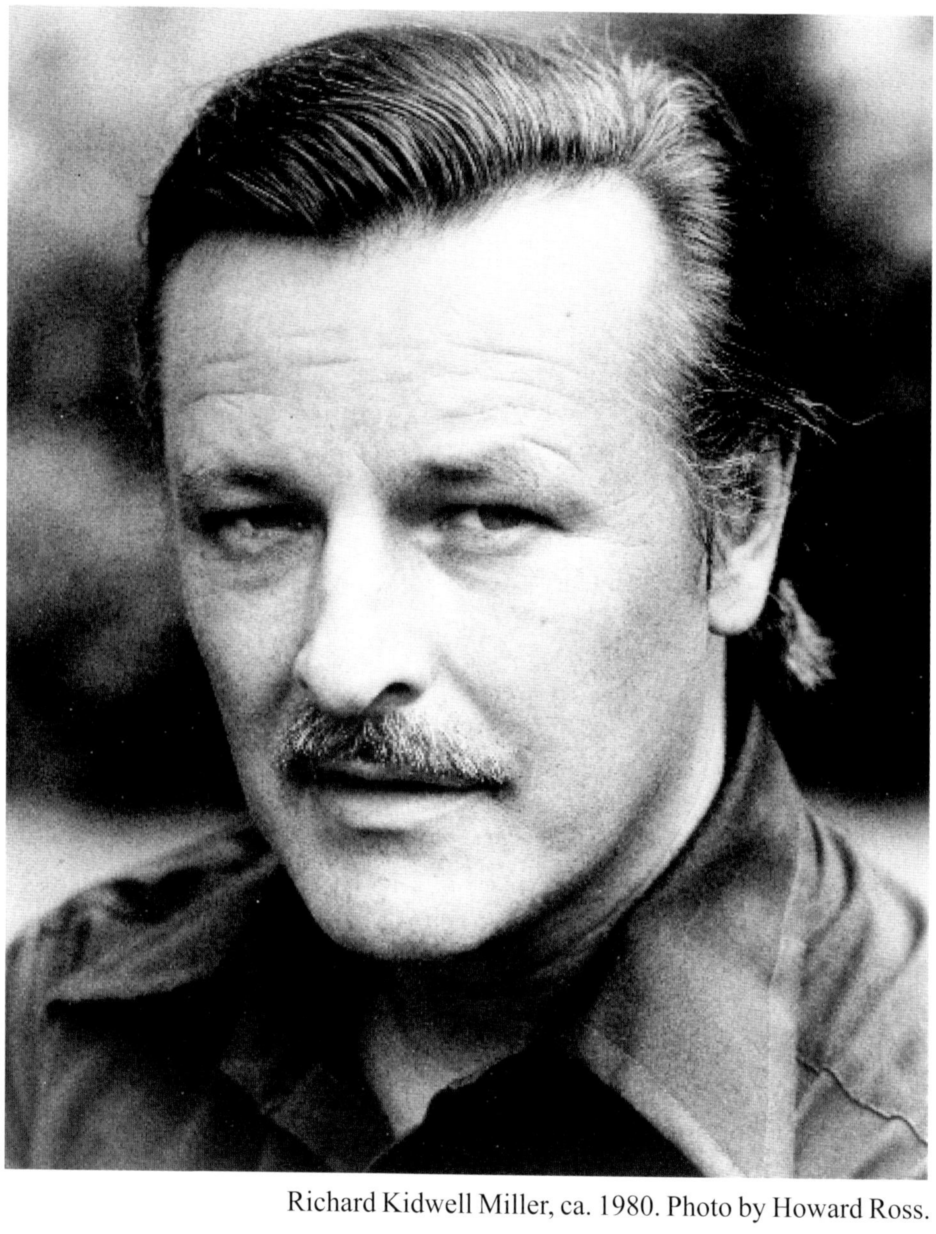

Richard Kidwell Miller, ca. 1980. Photo by Howard Ross.

The Art of Richard K. Miller: "What's Next?"

When Richard Miller received his first paint set at the age of six, little did anyone know that the young boy would one day be counted among the leading modern painters of his age. Due to his extraordinary precociousness and ambition, however, it did not take the world long to find out!

Born in Fairmont, West Virginia, in 1930, Miller grew up in a coal mining region in the midst of some of the worst economic times in the nation's history. Fortunately, Miller's father was able to spare his family the hardships suffered by many of their neighbors due to the stability of his employment with the local newspaper, and subsequently as proprietor of a job printing business, the Coal City Printing Company.[1]

The house in which the Miller family dwelled was situated near the city's center. Despite being 'in the heart of Appalachian coal country,' Miller recalls the home as being a 'typical' household that might have existed anywhere in America, 'cosmopolitan' even.

> *My parents were both highly literate and there was always an intellectual curiosity at home that extended to all things, from the latest news — my father worked for the newspaper, after all — to politics, literature and certainly also the arts, especially music. Our house was*

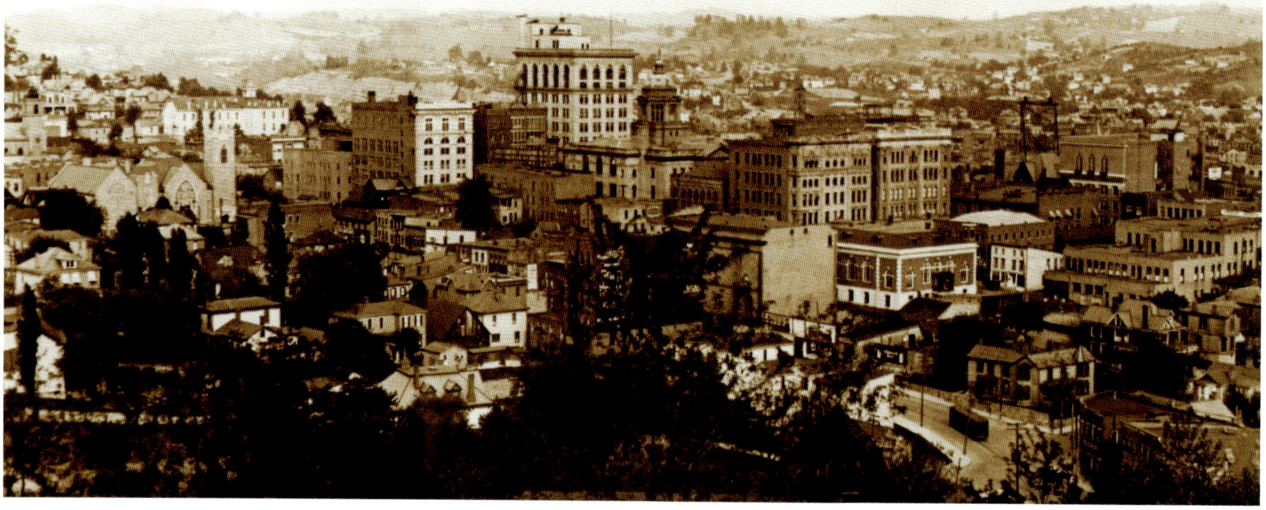

1. *Fairmont, West Virginia,* 1930. The Miller home is pictured at lower right immediately above the trolley car.

> *one of the primary gathering places for musicians in Fairmont. We hosted just about every big band that passed through the area.*[2]

Intellectual stimulation came also from Miller's two siblings who were both 'much older' than he, and 'exceptionally bright and successful.'

> *My brother was in law school at West Virginia University when I was still a small boy. He eventually practiced with Arnold and Porter in Washington, DC, one of the leading law firms in the country. My sister was married to Jess Speidel of Wheeling, a financier and philanthropist who became Vice President of the American Cancer Society.*

Considering such examples, it is not surprising that young Richard was both "in a hurry to grow up" and determined to "do something significant" with his life. It is unlikely, however, that the family took seriously his proclamation that he would become a great artist when he was still in the first grade. If so, they did not doubt it for long.

Miller still has in his possession his very first work — a pair of deer painted on an old window shade — produced with a "hand-me-down" paint set from his older brother. "I was thrilled with that painting...and I have never looked back."

The young artist's talents were discovered quickly upon his enrollment at the W.R. White School in Fairmont in 1936. Over the next several years he won numerous prizes for his work and also contributed much to the beautification of the school by contributing to murals that adorned the building's halls and classrooms.

Miller's first attempt at portraiture came when he was in the third grade:

> *An elderly, blind, black man lived in a shack under the Fairmont bridge [over the Monongahela River]. I asked him if I could paint his picture and he agreed. I set up my easel and painted the old gentleman seated on his porch. It was tremendously successful — for a nine year old.* [Plate 2]

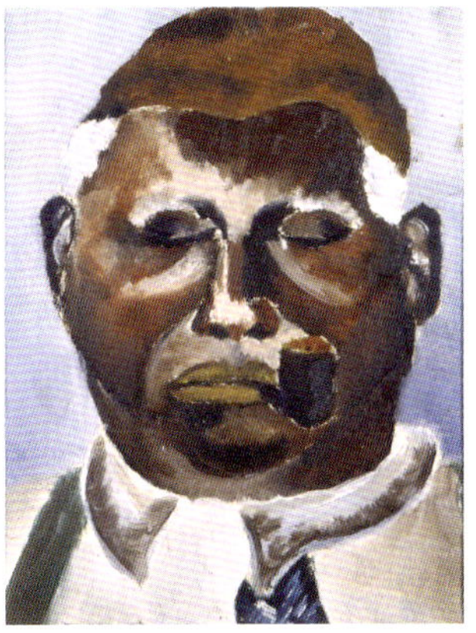

2. ***Portrait of Phil Johnson***, oil on canvas, 12 x 14 inches, 1939[3]

In 1939, a community art center opened in Fairmont. Funded by the Works Progress Administration, the Fairmont Art Center offered art lessons to all community residents without cost. A godsend, the center provided the aspiring artist with his first taste, or better yet, his first scent, of the world of the professional painter:

One of my fondest childhood memories is the smell of that studio — the smell of oil paint, turpentine, varnish, which is the smell of all studios — for me, that smell was heaven, a magical thing.

For the next three years, Richard attended "every possible" class at the center. Limited initially to after school and evening study, during the 5th and 6th grades he was granted early release from school each afternoon to attend the center.

Miller was fortunate not only for the Fairmont Art Center's existence, but also for the caliber of the instruction offered there by his teachers, who included the husband and wife team of Ernest B. Freed and Martha Himlich Freed.[4] Brought to Fairmont by a faculty appointment at Fairmont State College, Mr. Freed was extraordinarily well educated. His academic laurels included a pair of bachelors degrees from the University of Illinois, two years study at the Pennsylvania Academy for the Fine Arts, and a masters degree from the University of Iowa received under the tutelage of Grant Wood. The young Miller could not have had a better first teacher.

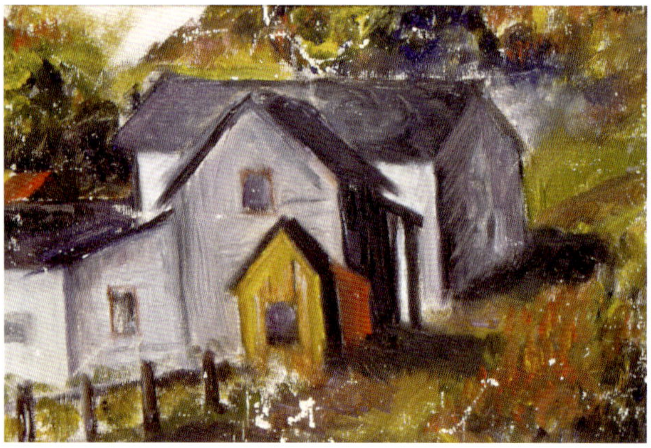

3. ***West Virginia Landscape***, oil on canvasboard, 9 x 12 inches, 1941

He was a marvelous instructor. He taught me a simplified way of drawing that I used for many years. I was sometimes very frustrated when I couldn't draw or paint as well as some of the adult students. I remember an older man whose drawings were superb. I wanted to be able to draw as well as he did. Ernest Freed taught me that drawing was really just learning to see. I have never forgotten that.

Miller also benefited from the 'progressive' nature of Freed's teaching:

During a portrait class I asked Mr. Freed how to paint the color of flesh. He responded by painting a complete portrait in greens to demonstrate that with the proper values, any color could function as flesh. Instruction like that was invaluable to me. It still is.

Yet another influence was Freed's own work which was "highly stylized" and "semi-abstract," reflecting the influence of his teacher, Grant Wood. Miller found it both "strange" and "exciting."

When Richard was ten years old, a ***Still Life*** painting he had recently completed was selected for an exhibition of juvenile art at the Metropolitan Museum of Art in New York. Another honor came the following year when a poster he designed for an annual war-time observance, "Poppy Day," won first prize in a contest sponsored by a local department store. Still in elementary school, Richard K. Miller's career was off and running.

4. ***"Willem Coymans" after Frans Hals***, oil on canvas, 27 x 22 inches,1946

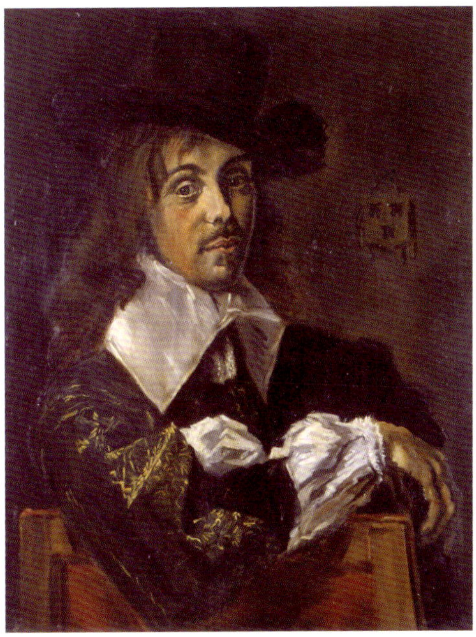

While the Great Depression gave birth to the Fairmont Arts Center, it proved to be the death of the Miller family printing business. By the early 1940s, what had begun two decades earlier as a highly prosperous enterprise was facing bankruptcy. Determined to provide for his family as best he could, in the spring of 1943, Miller's father made the decision to accept an offer of employment with the Government Printing Office in Washington, DC.

Thus, in June 1943, Richard Miller, who had never been in a museum or even seen a genuine painting other than by a fellow student or teacher, suddenly found himself in a museum mecca. He was soon frequenting the city's art museums, especially the National Gallery of Art where he quickly became a fixture. When he was granted permission to copy old master paintings at the National Gallery the following spring, he became the youngest artist ever to do so. He recalls working diligently that summer, from opening to closing each day, copying a work by a master that he particularly esteemed named 'van Rijn.' Several weeks went by before someone pointed out to him that the artist was better known by the first name, Rembrandt. Among his most successful efforts was a reproduction of a work by Frans Hals. (Plate 4)

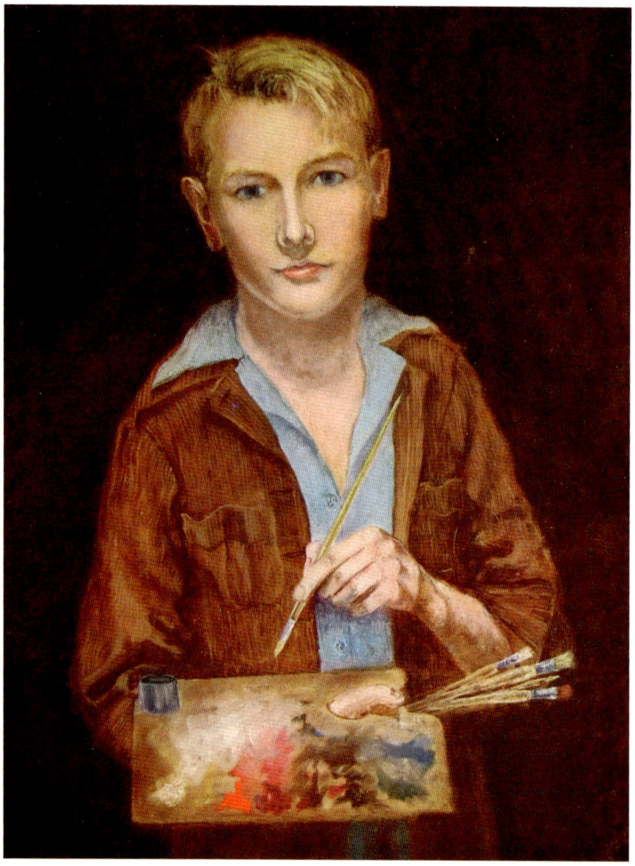

5. ***Self Portrait***, oil on canvas, approx. 32 x 24 inches, 1944. Collection of Mr. and Mrs. Reed Miller

In 1944, the ***Washington Times Herald*** inaugurated an annual open air art fair in the park behind the White House. The event included both art instruction and exhibitions, and offered a variety of prizes to participants. The 14-year-old West Virginian received his first critical acclaim at that event along with one of the festival's primary awards -- a scholarship to study privately with one of the city's foremost artists, William Howard Calfee.[5]

Mr. Calfee was a quiet, very intense man with an enormous degree of art in his soul. I attended his life drawing classes every Saturday. I believe my award,which was donated by Mr. Calfee, was for one year of study, but I continued going to those classes for several years. I was always welcome.

Miller won a second prestigious scholarship from the ***Washington Times Herald*** at the following year's festival: a grant for a full summer of study with Henry Henche at the celebrated Cape Cod School of Art in Provincetown, Massachusetts.[6]

> *[Provincetown] was an incredible experience, especially for someone my age. The whole town was alive with galleries and studios. Hans Hofmann's studio was just down the street from where I stayed, though I don't think I knew it at the time.... I rented a cellar with another student. The scholarship paid my tuition, but we lived on next to nothing. We would go down to the docks in the evening and yell to the fishing boats as they came in, and they'd throw us a fish. That was our supper.*

While the ***Washington Times Herald*** contributed much to financing the budding artist's early education, it was the ***Washington Post***, that earned the distinction of being Miller's first publisher. In the fall of 1944, the newspaper organized an art contest for the area's high school population. From among the many entries that flooded in, four winning works were selected for reproduction in the annual ***Washington Post Calendar*** for the coming year. Among them was Richard Miller's ***Self Portrait***. (Plate 5)

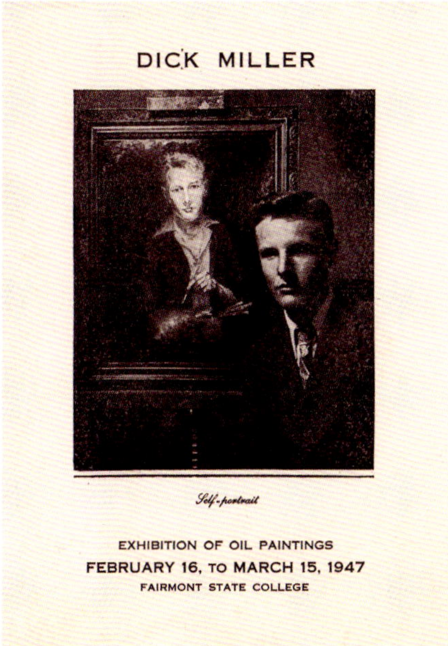

6. ***Dick Miller***, exhibit brochure cover, Fairmont State College, 1947

By 1947, Miller was showing his paintings in most of the juried exhibitions in the Washington area. Still just a junior in high school, his budding career did not escape notice back in Fairmont. On February 16 of that year, the Miller family returned to West Virginia to attend the opening of the young painter's first one-man show, an exhibition of 11 portraits, at Fairmont State College. Organized by the College Community Art Association and Junior League of Fairmont, the exhibit proved captivating to "a large number of admiring" viewers, according to the local newspaper.[7]

Back in Washington the following spring, when one of

Miller's works was included in a group show of Washington artists at the White Gallery, it captivated one of the foremost art connoisseurs in the nation, Duncan Phillips. Descended from a family whose fortune was forged in the Pittsburgh steel mills, Phillips' father, Duncan Phillips Sr., relocated his family in the nation's capital shortly before the turn of the 20th century to be closer to the center of national culture and politics. It was his untimely death, as well as that of Duncan Jr.'s brother, James, that led to the establishment of the 'Phillips Memorial Gallery' in the family's Georgian Revival home at 1600 21st Street in Washington in 1918.

By the late 1940s, the Phillips Collection, was recognized as one of the nation's great art museums, and a leading venue for modern art. The 18-year-old Miller, not yet out of high school, found himself in good company when his painting, ***Love Match,*** was exhibited there in 1948 at Mr. Phillips' personal request.

> *My work was primarily figurative at that time, but very modern and very unique. Mr. Phillips commented that this was what he found so appealing about it — its originality. 'Don't ever change,' he advised me. But how can you expect an 18-year-old not to change?*

Miller eventually came to know Phillips well:

> *He was the epitome of an urbane gentleman — polite, reserved. Yet despite his quiet demeanor he was almost intimidating in his persona due to his position as one of the two or three greatest art collectors in the world at the time.*

The Phillips Collection, in fact, became something of a "second home" for Miller in the ensuing years. He eventually received part-time employment there, "sitting on the door," in

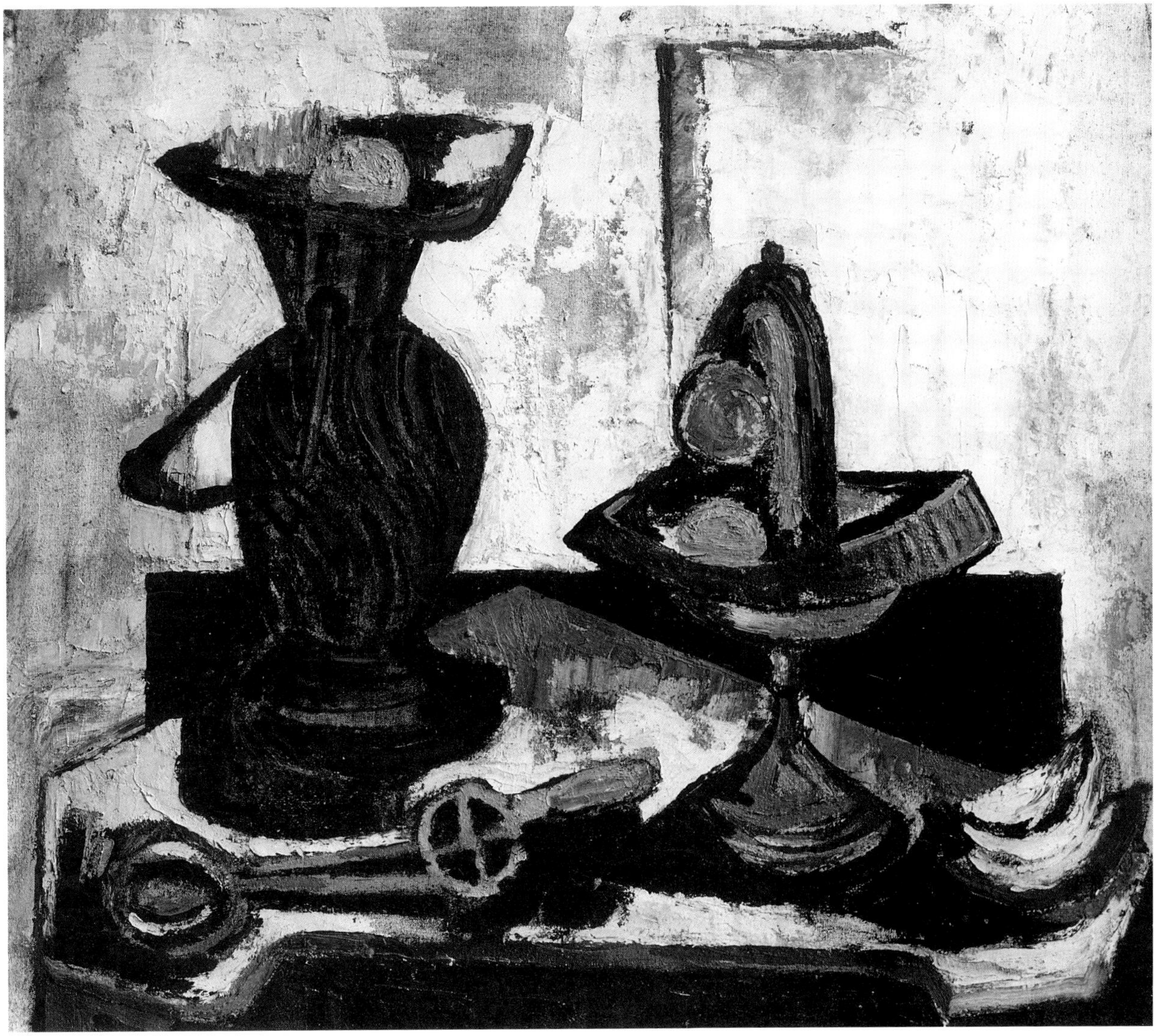

7. ***Egg Beater and Urn***, oil on canvas, 24 x 30 inches, 1953. Phillips Collection, Washington, DC

the evenings as well as an invitation to work in the "wonderful" studio space that then existed on the building's fourth floor. "And when I wasn't working there in one capacity or another, I was usually hanging out with the staff and crowd that congregated there."

Upon graduating from Anacostia High School in June 1948, Miller received one of the most lucrative prizes available to aspiring artists of the day, the Gertrude Vanderbilt Whitney scholarship. Awarded by the Washington Chapter of the National Society of Arts and Letters, the prize provided funds for up to five years of study at the college level. "Receiving that scholarship was an incredible thrill," Miller recollects, "because there was no way my family could have afforded to put me through college at that time."

Miller spent the first year of his scholarship at the Pennsylvania Academy for the Fine Arts in Philadelphia but found the institution "too conservative" and "stifling."

> *It was incredibly conservative. By then I was fascinated by Modigliani, and the modern French school, especially Picasso and Braque. They barely acknowledged the fact that those artists existed. Today the school is far better.*

He remembers spending most of that year visiting the Philadelphia Museum of Art and doing a great deal of "independent study." When the school year ended, he returned home to Washington. That fall, he transferred his credits to American University where his former teacher and mentor William Calfee headed the art department. He spent the next three and a half years there, working under Calfee, Robert Gates and Sarah Baker, with "great satisfaction."

In addition to his occasional work at the Phillips Collection, Miller supplemented his income while attending college by assisting in the restoration of the large history paintings in the Rotunda of the United States Capitol Building. Working under the direction of the conservators of the esteemed Veerhoff Galleries, the experience afforded him with an opportunity to learn a great deal about the science of painting and the importance of conservationally sound materials to the longevity of his artwork.

Miller's musical talents also helped pay the bills during this period:

I studied singing and appeared in a number of amateur theater productions when I was in high school. When I found out that the Episcopal Church across from the White House was hiring singers I went right over. I worked as a baritone soloist there on and off for the next several years. Harry Truman was frequently in the first row.

Miller's artwork drew increasing accolades during his college years and was routinely included in the city's leading venues. His return to the local exhibition circuit from Philadelphia in 1949 was rewarded with a gold medal in the field of portrait painting at the Society of Washington Artists' annual exhibition at the Smithsonian Institution that fall. Other medals followed in the ensuing years. At a Corcoran Gallery exhibit in 1953, his ***Egg Beater and Urn*** (Plate 7) won not one, but two prizes: a first prize for still life painting and a third prize for "best painting in show." One of the work's greatest admirers was Duncan Phillips who promptly purchased the piece for the Phillips Collection.

8. ***The Accordian Player,*** oil on canvas, 56 x 40 inches, Paris, 1953

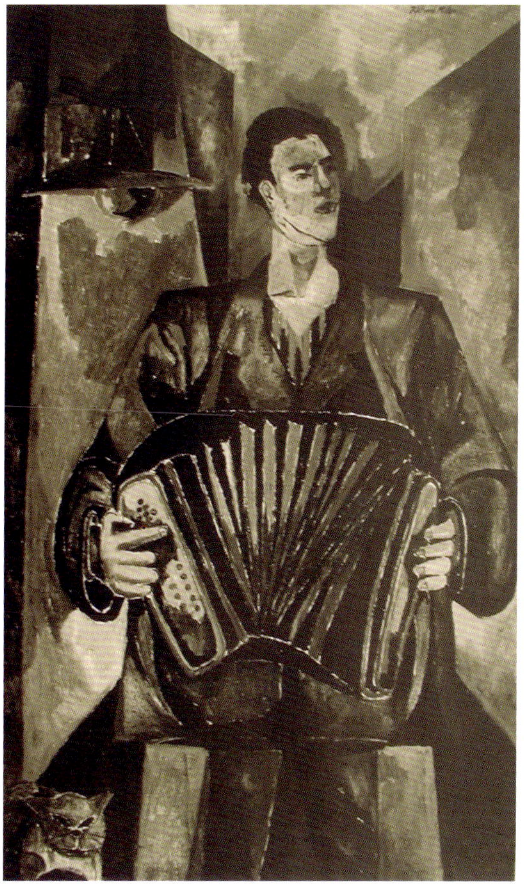

Upon graduating from American University in May, 1953, Miller received yet another prestigious scholarship, a Fulbright Fellowship funding a year's study abroad. Settling in Paris, he would spend as much time looking at art as creating it during the year that followed. "It was my first opportunity to study firsthand the works of the modern European masters I had admired for many years, and an opportunity to find new ones."

It was on a side trip to England that he discovered an affinity between his own work and that of the English master Graham Sutherland. "I was fascinated by the way he would take ordinary objects and blow them up making them monumental." After seeing a giant grasshopper by Sutherland, Miller was inspired to paint a ten-foot ***Homard (Lobster)***.

Another painter whose work struck a special chord was Georges Braque:

> *Braque was a genius when it came to organization — the intelligence he used in composing his work, the muted coloration, his textures, they all appealed to me. And his use of collage — it was Braque who invented collage. Picasso picked up on it and ran with it, like he did with the ideas of so many other artists, but it was Braque's invention.*

In his own work, Miller spent his time "sorting through" the many influences he encountered, while endeavoring to retain the originality that Duncan Phillips had praised so highly several years earlier. He considered the acceptance of one of his paintings for exhibition in the prestigious Salon de National at the Musee d'Art Moderne to be an indication of his success.

Miller's artistic adventures in Paris became unexpectedly diversified when a writer friend from Philadelphia suggested one day that he join him in auditioning for 'extra' work in a French film that was in production in the Paris suburb of Neuilly. Though such work proved unavailable on that particular day, Miller learned that English speaking actors were then being sought by the French National Radio for a series of plays on "the great men of France" for distribution to English speaking countries. Miller wound up performing in more than a dozen productions in the ensuing months as well as dubbing assorted parts for three French films. He also joined the choir of the American Cathedral on Avenue Georges Cinq.

Richard K. Miller was clearly among the most promising young painters in the Washington area when he returned from Europe in the summer of 1954. The Franz Bader Gallery marked his homecoming by offering him a one man show that fall. Several months later, he learned that his work had been selected for an even more prestigious exhibit — a solo show at the Baltimore Museum of Art.

It was quite an honor for an artist my age. I had a very large gallery with a number of paintings. The biggest piece was bought by Edward Joseph Gallagher who bequeathed it to the University of Arizona Museum where it resides today. (Plate 9)

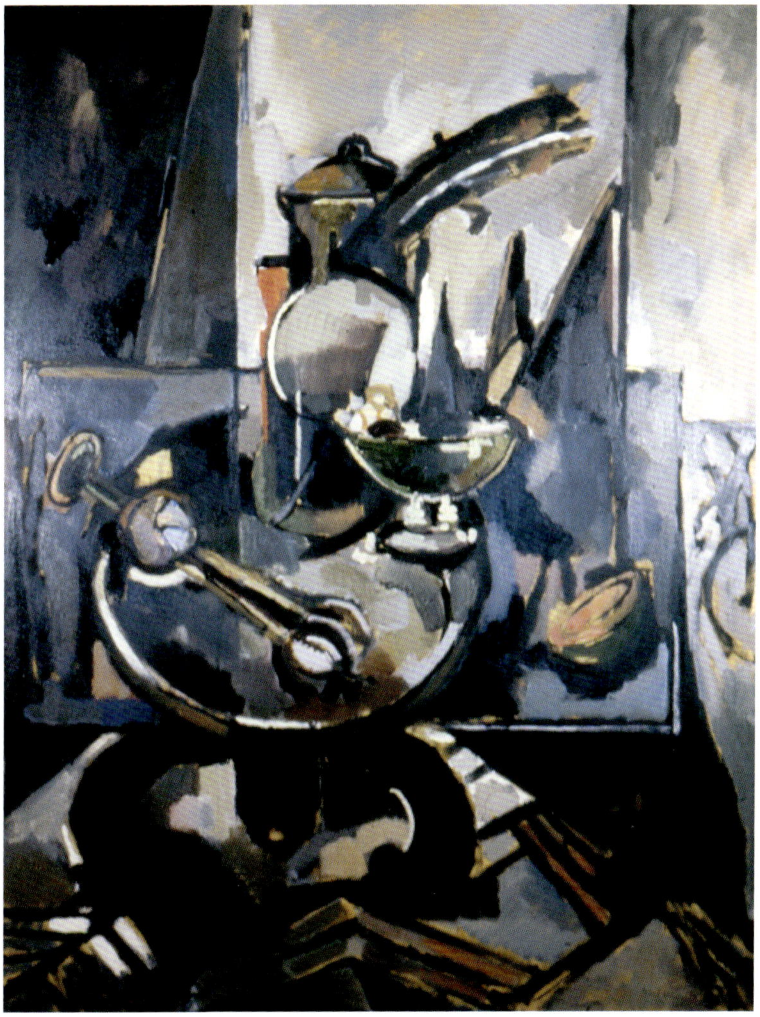

9. ***Interior***, oil on canvas, 56 x 44 inches, 1955.Collection of the University of Arizona Museum of Art, Tucson, AZ. Gift of Edward J. Gallagher, Jr.

While working on the two exhibits, to make ends meet, Miller accepted a job teaching in the Washington public schools during the winter of 1954/1955. Somehow, he found additional time to continue his studies, via night classes, with his favorite American University teacher, William Calfee.

The following spring, Miller received an invitation to visit Sarah Baker's summer studio on Nantucket Island. Thoroughly enchanted by the place, he decided to remain on the island for the entire summer. This proved to be a pivotal moment in his artistic development:

> *A lot of things began to happen in my work on Nantucket. The objects in my still lifes suddenly wanted to move. They just wouldn't stay still.... That was when I truly began to turn into an abstract painter; the handling of the paint was very expressionistic, loose, free, and very abstract in quality. It was the design of the painting that interested me; emotion came through the design and the handling, and not through any story. I've been that kind of painter ever since.*

The art critic for the Nantucket ***Inquirer and Mirror*** expressed his approval of the advances Miller made that summer by proclaiming that his entry "stole the show" at the Nantucket art colony's annual exhibit in August.

Exhilarated by his new momentum, and with mounting professional successes under his belt, that summer Miller made the decision to establish himself in the center of the international art world, New York City. With renewed assistance from the Gertrude Vanderbilt Whitney scholarship, supplemented by a job as baritone soloist at St. Thomas Church on Fifth Avenue, he enrolled in the Master of Fine Arts program at Columbia University that fall. It was during this period, he now recognizes, that he first began to reach maturity as a painter.

> *I was required to paint a one-man show as my thesis. This took the form of a series of very large still lifes. I began with a careful study of the still lifes of the Dutch masters,using actual reproductions of their paintings to borrow the composition elements that appealed to me. This became a very successful series of paintings for me and broke the early influences such as Cubism and the*

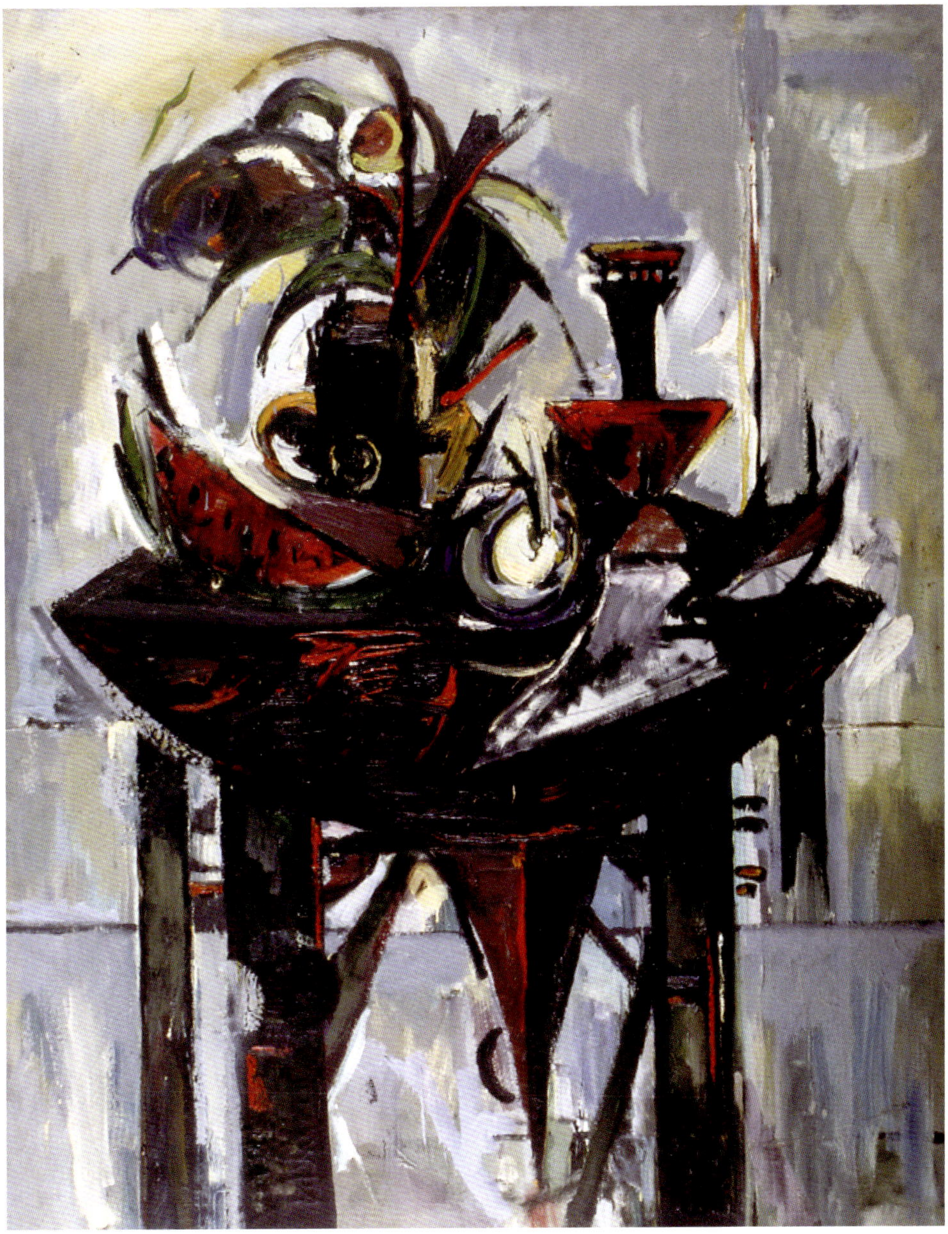

10. ***Table with 3 Legs***, oil on canvas, 56 x 44 inches, 1956

> *other early loves.... It was very strong work and a few were highly original.* (Plate 10)

Receiving his MFA degree in May, Miller devoted the summer of 1956 to exploring an artistic adventure of a different sort:

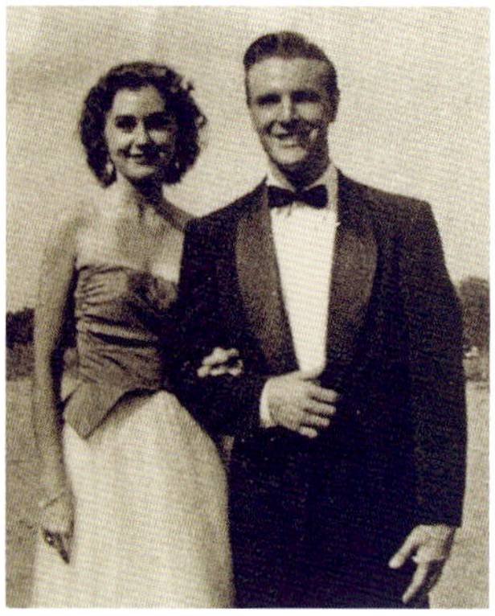

11. *Teresa Robinson and Richard Miller outside the Finger Lakes Lyric Theater, 1956*

I used to room with a couple of guys who were both in theater and when they heard that I had sung professionally and also done a good bit of radio theater work they urged me to start auditioning with them for various jobs around town. I ended up landing a position with a summer stock company in upstate New York that summer, in the Finger Lakes area. It was a thoroughly delightful experience.

Miller's first professional stint on stage yielded more than just wages. That summer he became enamored with a fellow cast member, "a very talented and beautiful singer," named Teresa Robinson. The two were married the following spring.

Critical acclaim for Miller's work continued upon his return to New York City. When he was invited to exhibit at the Whitney Annual that fall along with some of America's leading painters — Charles Burchfield, Robert Motherwell, Georgia O'Keefe, Larry Rivers, Ad Reinhardt, Max Weber — "many of whom became good friends," a New Yorker critic deemed his entry, ***Grey Still Life***, (Plate 12) to be one of the best in the show.

Miller received an invitation from Whitney director Lloyd Goodridge to exhibit at the museum again in 1957. Titled "Fulbright Painters at the Whitney," that exhibit proceeded to tour 19 museums across the nation following its New York debut.

When the newly-wed Millers moved into an eight-room apartment on East 96th St. later that year, they discovered that their neighbors included Mark Rothko, Robert Motherwell, Helen Frankenthaler, Giorgio Cavallon, and a young Japanese painter named James Suzuki.

I had known Suzuki in Washington, and we became very

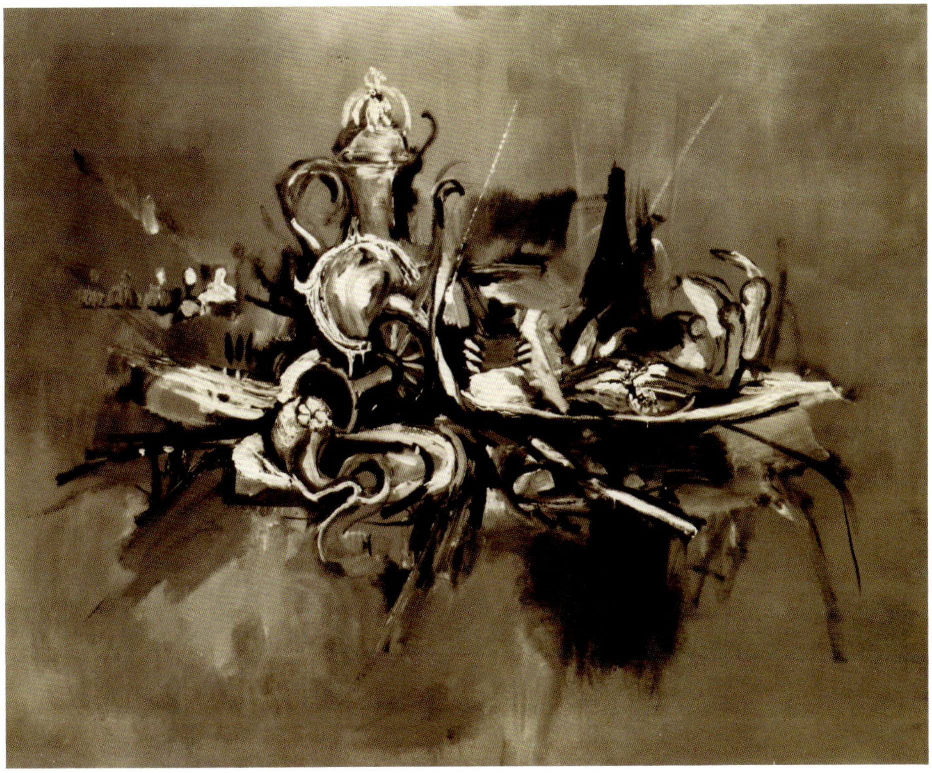

12. ***Grey Still Life***, oil on canvas, 44 x 56 inches, 1956 Private collection

good friends in New York. He was extremely successful and was showing at the Duveen Graham Gallery, one of New York's well-known Madison Avenue galleries. He recommended me to the gallery and they soon included one of my works in a group show. It was picked out by a ***New York Times*** *critic as the best painting in the show. A short time later, Joseph Hirschhorn bought a painting of mine at the gallery that ended up in the Hirschhorn Museum and Sculpture Garden in Washington, DC.*

Miller received his first solo show at the Graham Gallery in 1960. The event proved to be a resounding success. "The reviews were excellent and a number of paintings were sold," he recalls. A ***New York Times*** critic praised especially the artist's cerebral approach to organizing abstract forms. "They have the intellectuality of a Braque...as they proceed to solve formal problems that are anything but simple."[8] Other successful shows would follow at the Graham Gallery with which the artist

13. ***Strata***, oil on canvas, 108 x 57 inches, 1960

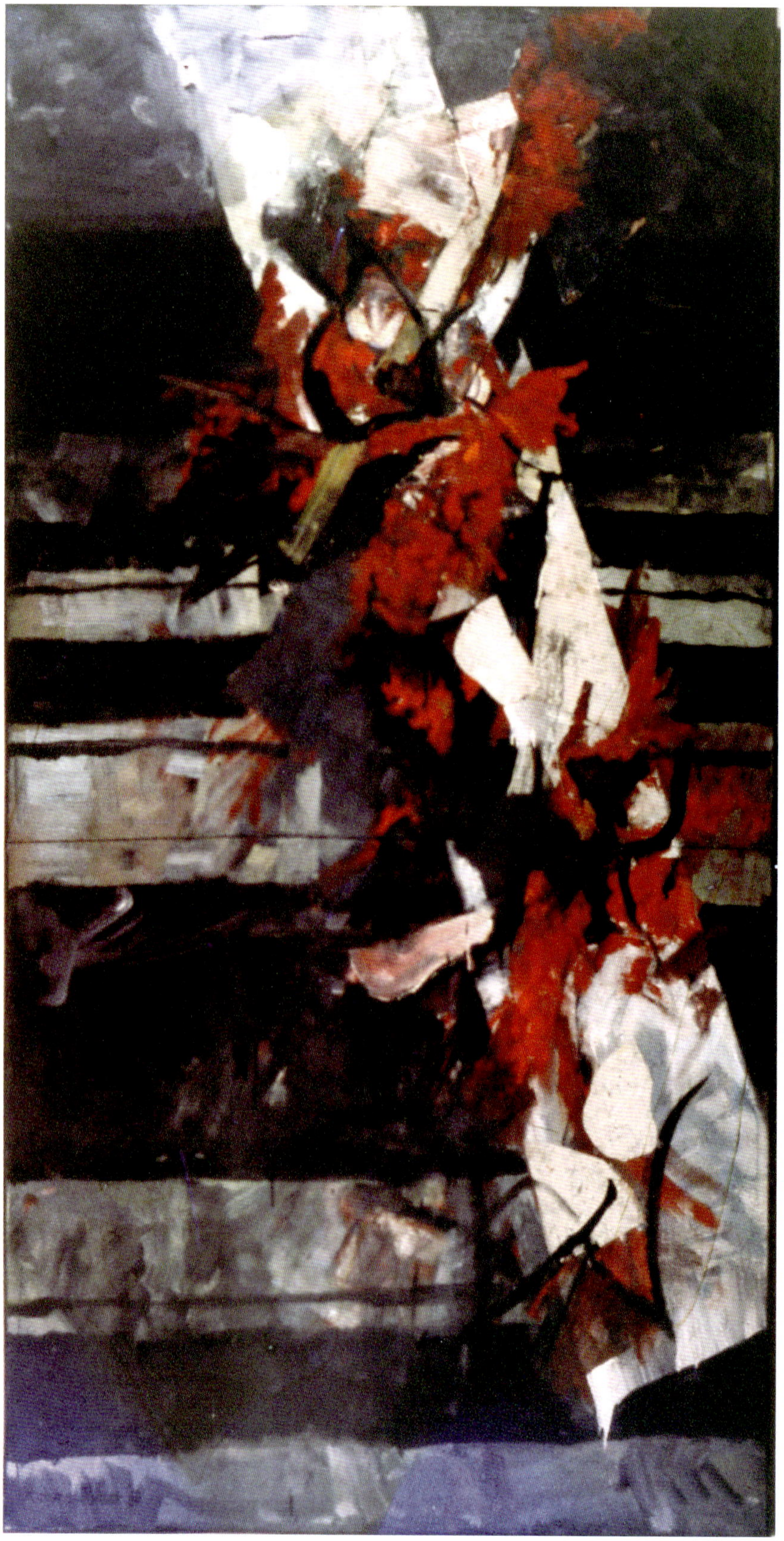

remained affiliated for the next ten years.

Miller considers the pinnacle of his many early successes to be his invitation to participate in the Carnegie International in 1961. Out of more than 300 paintings submitted by the foremost artists of 29 countries, Miller's ***Strata*** was selected as one of the International's top 21 paintings. (Plate 13) A striking work featuring strong horizontal and diagonal bands of intense color, with elements of collage thrown in for textural variety, the painting was reproduced in ***Art International*** alongside a work by Jasper Johns.[9]

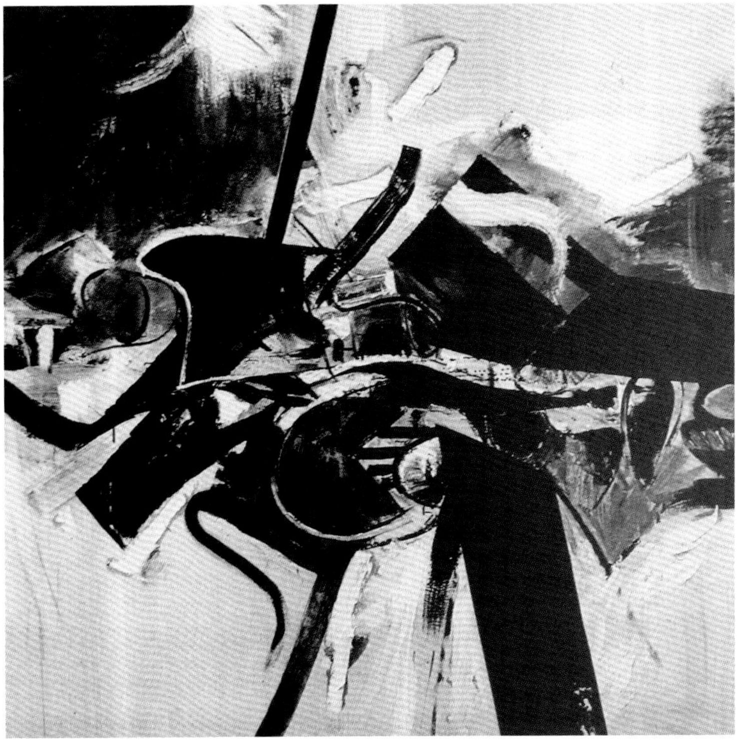

14. ***Triple Bar Form***, oil on canvas, 68 x 68 inches, 1963

As the 1960s progressed, Miller's paintings grew increasingly abstract. When the ***New York Herald Tribune's*** John Greun encountered his latest work at the Graham Gallery in 1963, he was struck by the "strong, almost brutal abstraction" and "supercharged" nature of paintings such as ***Triple Bar Form,*** which the celebrated critic deemed to be of "uncommon beauty."[10] (Plate 14)

Despite such accolades, Miller would soon veer sharply away from the large spontaneous expressionist pieces that had quickly brought him a measure of fame. The three-dimensionality rendered by the collage elements that he had begun incorporating in his work propelled him in a new direction during the mid-1960s. In just a few years time, broad free brush strokes gave way to orderly constructions created on canvas with a precisionist, neo-plastic bent. Though these new works bore

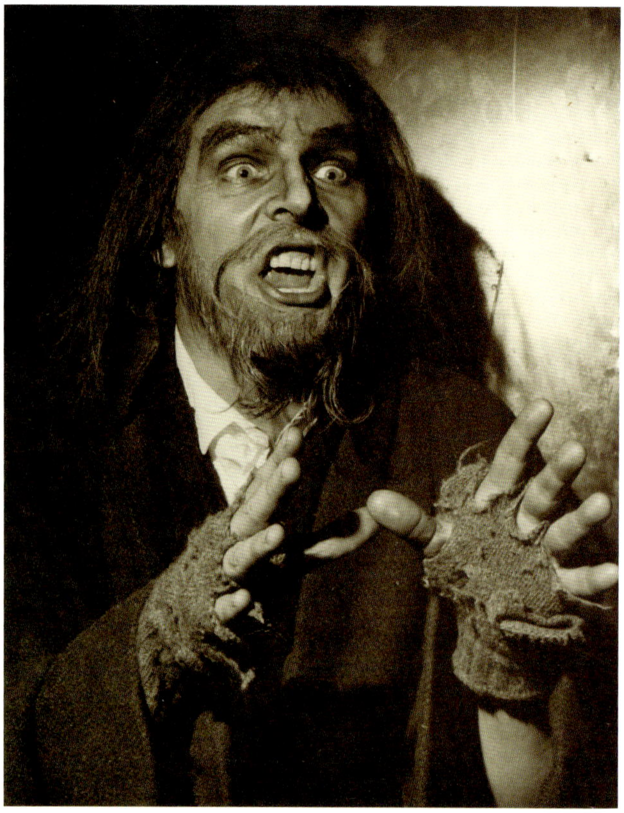

15. Richard Miller as "Fagin" in the Broadway musical ***Oliver***, ca. 1965, photo by Edward J. Avery

little resemblance to the spontaneous appearance of his expressionist paintings, the process of making them was essentially the same: "I approached the creation of these works the same way I always had, through hit or miss, trial and error, building up, tearing down, eliminating, erasing."

Throughout these years, the Millers continued to be active in the theater, in both plays and musicals, on and off Broadway. The couple appeared together in the long-running Broadway production of ***Oliver***, and traveled about the state and country with stock theater companies on several occasions. Teresa eventually joined the chorus of the Metropolitan Opera where she sang alongside Pavarotti and other Metropolitan Opera greats regularly.[11] Miller insists that his theater work did not detract from his painting but was interwoven with, and inspirational to it. "I was always painting up a storm backstage wherever we went and having a marvelous time doing it. If we were scheduled to spend more than a week in a town , I rented studio space and worked on major paintings."

By the mid 1960s, the Millers' Upper East Side apartment had become a popular gathering place for artists, actors and opera singers from across the city. Parties in their home routinely drew "more than 100 guests ranging from Paul Burlin to Albert Finney."

Miller recalls that another favorite social haunt of the New York art crowd during this period was the Cedar Bar near Washington Square.

On almost any given night you could find Kline, de Kooning, Guston, Burlin, Newman and most of the rest of the Abstract Expressionists there. Also about 500 young artists, myself included, all rubbing shoulders with the greats.

Miller continued to experience much critical acclaim through the late 1960s, not only in the gallery, but on the stage as well. In 1968, already juggling two careers, he was intrigued when he received an offer to embark on yet a third — a position on the faculty at the Kansas City Art Institute, one of the nation's finest art schools.

One of the professors was going on sabbatical that year and they asked me to fill in for him. I accepted and discovered that I really enjoyed teaching. I might have had an opportunity to stay there permanently if I wasn't dead set on returning to New York which was, and is, the center of the world to me.

16. ***Juggernaut***, acrylic and wood on canvas, 25 x 25 inches, 1972

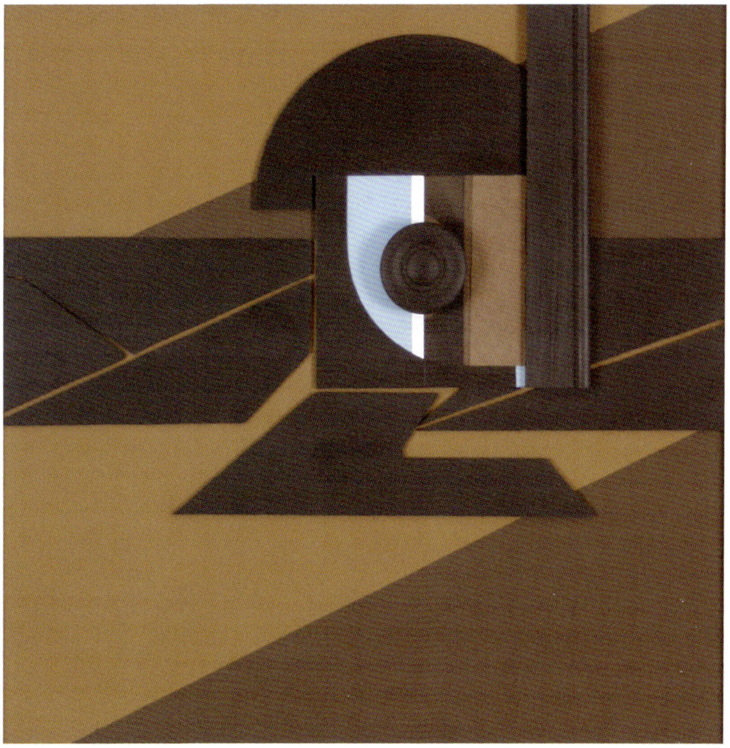

In the years that followed, Miller found ample opportunity to teach closer to home. In 1970, he was invited to join the faculty at the Scarsdale Studio School where his colleagues included Theodoros Stamos, and several other well known painters. When the school closed its doors in 1973, other opportunities came including posts at the Westchester Community College and the JCC of Mid-Westchester, where he continues to teach to this day.

Due to his many competing interests, advancing age, and with eight Broadway shows under his belt, Miller gradually withdrew from the stage during the mid-1970s. "Something had to give way," he recalls.

> *I was teaching regularly, painting everyday — I was affiliated with Aaron Berman Gallery at the time. The theater work, though I loved it dearly, became increasingly draining. I began to realize that I had to make choices. And painting will always be my first love.*

The constant evolution that had always characterized Miller's work continued as the years passed. During the late 1970s, he concentrated his efforts on the production of medium-sized works incorporating three dimensional objects made of cork, wood and metal, which were glued into his canvases to create the sensations of weight, balance and mystery. (Plate16) In an interview in the ***Greenwich Village News***, he stated that the ultimate motivation behind these works was "an attempt to achieve a kind of order on canvas" that he felt was lacking, both in his own life, and in an age which was devoid of the order provided by religion, and intellectual and political movements in the past.[12]

In 1981, Miller was invited to participate in a unique group exhibition, dedicated to exploring the creative process, at the Alternative Mueum in the SoHo area of Lower Manhattan. Titled, "Ambiance/Stimuli," the exhibition, curated by Benny Andrews, sought to expose the "means," rather than the "end," in the creation of art by revealing the "symbols, images and found objects" from which the ideas of the participating artists emanated. Miller's installation was composed of sand, pebbles, and rocks, a photo assemblage of cloud and geologic forms, and a 14-foot three-dimensional charcoal drawing on canvas. (Plate 17) In his artist's statement, Miller explained that while his

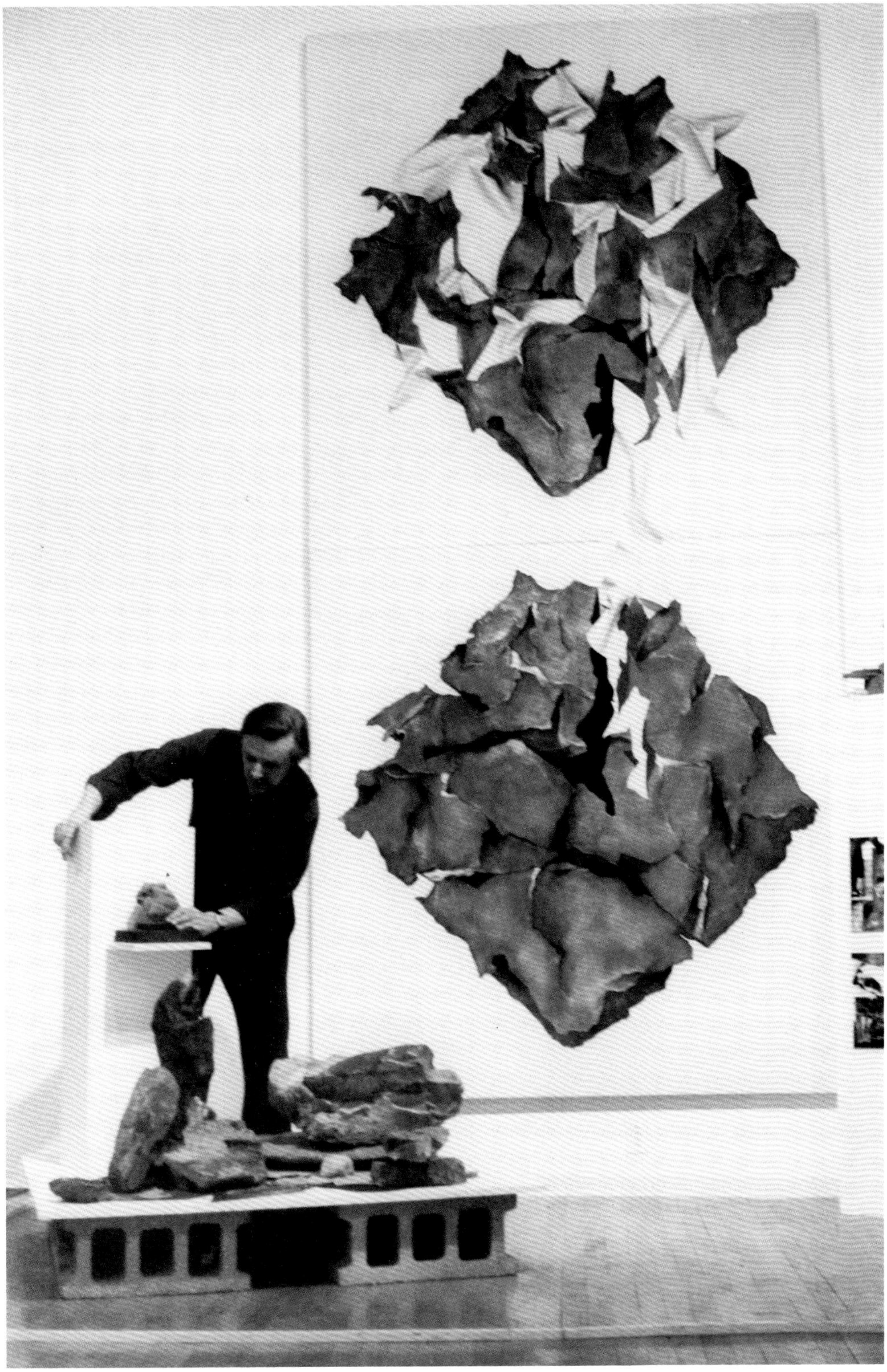

17. Miller adjusts his *Ambiance Stimuli* installation, at the Alternative Museum, New York, 1982.

paintings may not look like rocks, "collecting rocks leads to drawings, and then paintings." In a review of the exhibit, artist/critic Martin Ries stated that the ambiance/stimuli he perceived in contemplating Miller's installation included "solidity, unity, strength and integrity."[13] Such terms have frequently been applied to Miller's art.

During the mid-1980s, Miller returned to representational art when he began to sense that his abstract work was becoming "predictable." He ended up traveling "full circle," back to a form that had fascinated him since his youth — the still life. His ability to draw upon insights and technical advances learned over the preceding quarter century resulted in a series of highly crafted, monumental paintings that he still considers "without question some of my strongest work." (Plate 18) Critics agreed. In a lengthy 1988 article in ***American Artist***, the painter/writer Eunice Agar extolled the extraordinary energy and power of Miller's latest works, praising especially the artist's ability to forge a novel fusion of abstract and representational forms, due to his "equal familiarity with both styles," and thorough grounding in the history of painting:

> *A major problem with contemporary art in every style is its superficiality. Although competently painted, much representational art, especially that which depicts still life, is simply decoration. Similarly, abstract styles have degenerated into repeatable formulas. But there are few artists who have been able to combine avant-garde concepts, especially the new dynamics of form and color, with techniques of historical realism to present a new revitalized representational art. In the process we may find it necessary to relearn the value of many years work. That concept of time produced the Old Master painters, but is inimical to our quick-fix approach to knowledge.*[14]

Despite such acclaim, Miller's return to representation

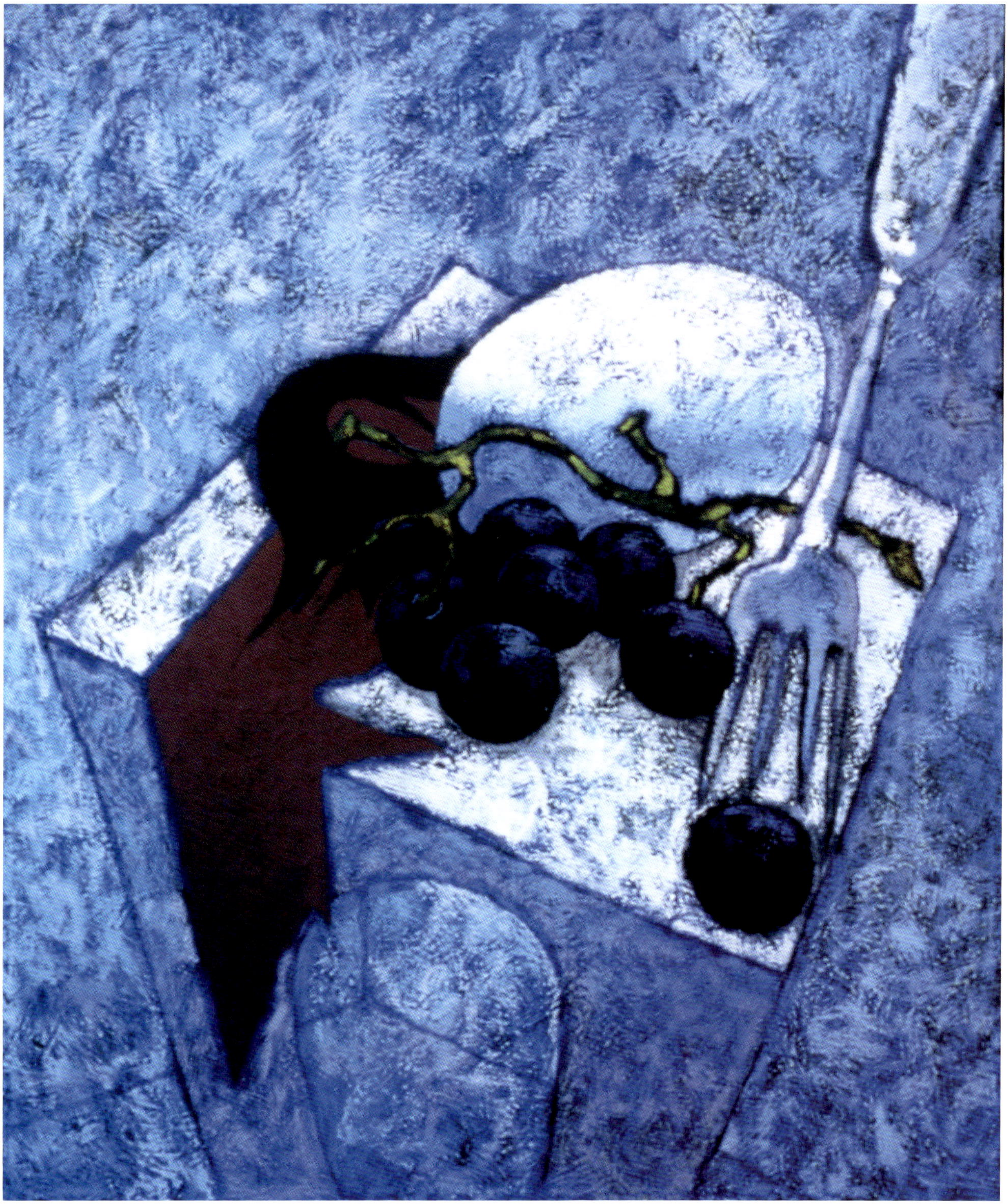

18. ***Still Life***, oil and oil stick on canvas, 80 x 69 inches, 1983

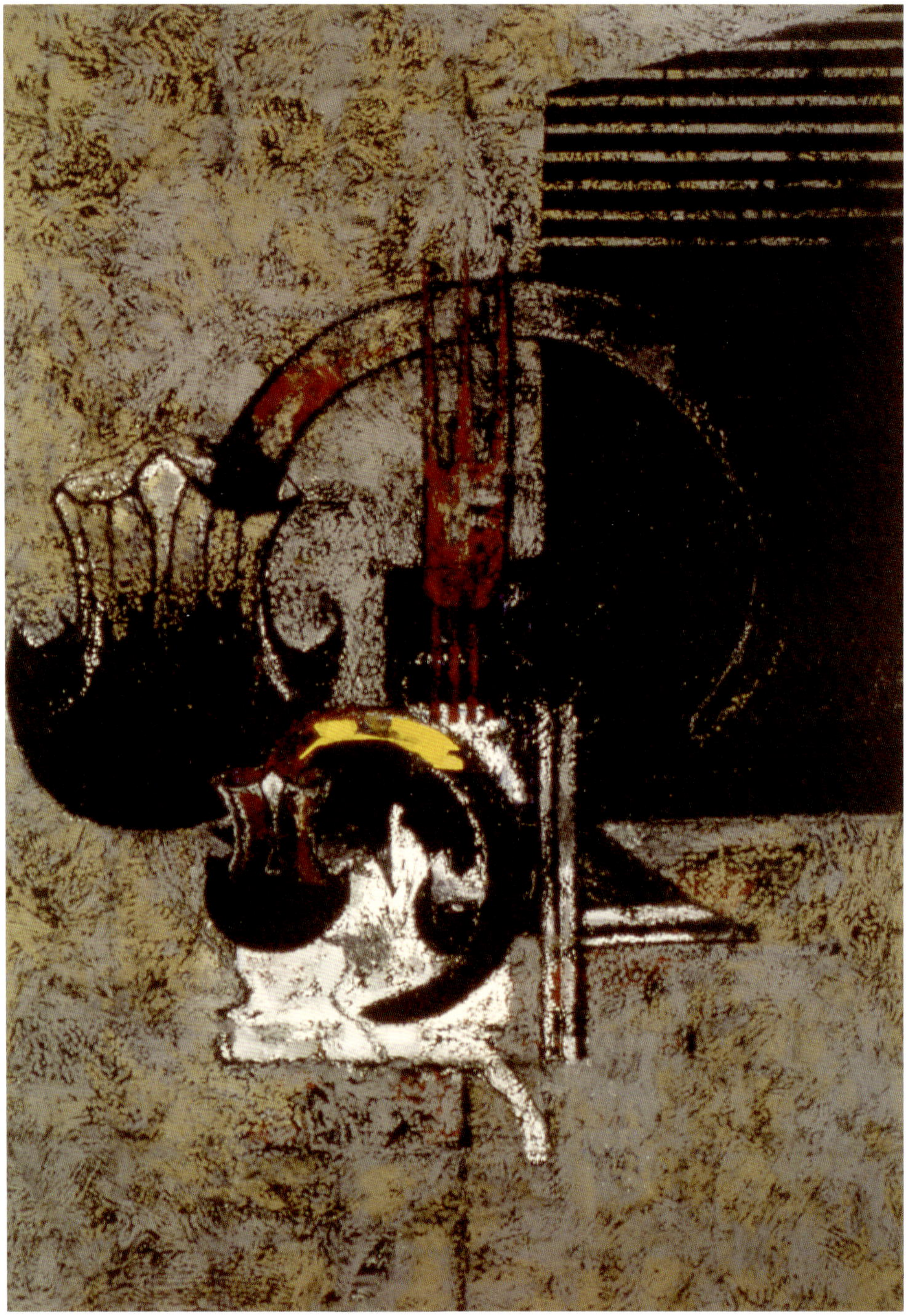

19. ***The Second Source***, oil and oil stick on canvas, 80 x 56 inches, 2001

proved to be relatively short-lived:

> *My semi-abstract still lifes eventually developed into a form of completely realized still life that was new for me. The evolution was due in part to my discovery of an*

entirely new method of painting using paint sticks which gave my work a graphic intensity and marvelous textured surface that was a real breakthrough.

As I worked on these paintings, my thinking was that this oil stick technique was a great one for doing abstract work and so I began to gradually shift back in that direction.

The return to abstraction about 1989 led Miller to resume his lifelong study of abstract form, both across time and across cultures. A new world opened up to him when he began sketching African and Native American designs at the Metropolitan Museum of Art and Indian Museum. He went on to discover that the incorporation of "primitive" concepts in his formal language imbued his work with an elemental, emotional, even spiritual, quality that was absent from his earlier abstract paintings.

In an article published in the ***Christian Science Monitor*** in June, 1990, Theodore F. Wolff praised the latest incarnation of Miller's art as "profoundly moving in substance and mood." Having followed the artist's career through many vicissitudes over several decades, the noted critic lauded Miller's ever-greater "formal control and expressive clout" and perpetual progressive momentum:

Unlike contemporaries who make desperate attempts to "update" the work that won them some measure of fame 10, 20, possibly even 40 years ago, Miller sticks by his guns and improves steadily.... The result is a body of work that is rock-solid in integrity.... Shown one-on-one, without prejudices, his best canvases would hold up well against almost anyone's today.[15]

Wolff's assessment included a prediction, based upon "the glimpse I've had of an unfinished work," that Richard Miller's best work was yet to come.

In the intervening thirteen years, Miller has, indeed, created some of the most powerful and stirring works of his career, a fact to which the recent paintings in the present exhibit attest. At age 73, he continues to approach the art of painting each day with the same enthusiasm he had when he first touched brush to window shade nearly seven decades ago. "Unpredictability," he insists, is the key.

What's next? Not even Richard Kidwell Miller knows!

Notes

[1] Maurice E. Miller worked as a proofreader for ***The West Virginian***. Prior to founding the Coal City Printing Company about 1920, he was also employed as a foreman at the Fairmont Printing and Lithography Company.

[2] Quotations from Richard Miller which appear throughout this essay are drawn from several sources. Most have come directly from the artist through personal interviews. Others have been borrowed, sometimes in modified form with the artist's approval, from the biographical sources listed in the bibliography.

[3] All artworks reproduced in the present catalogue are in the personal collection of the artist unless otherwise indicated in photo captions.

[4] Ernest Bradfield Freed (1908-1974). For more information on this artist see John A. Cuthbert. ***Early Art and Artists in West Virginia***. Morgantown, WV: WVU Press, 2000; Peter Hastings Falk, ***Who Was Who in American Art***, Madison, CT: Soundview Press, 1999. Vol. I, 1188.

[5] William Howard Calfee (B. 1909) For more information on this artist see Peter Hastings Falk, ***Who Was Who in American Art***, Madison, CT: Soundview Press, 1999. Vol. I, 543.

[6] Henry Hensche (1901-1992). For more information on this artist see Peter Hastings Falk, ***Who Was Who in American Art***, Madison, CT: Soundview Press, Vol. II 1535.

[7] Three short articles concerning the exhibit and related society news appear in ***The West Virginian,*** on February 16 and 17, 1947.

[8] ***New York Times***, 1960. Undated clipping in the possession of the artist.

[9] ***Art International***, IV, 1961.

[10] ***New York Herald Tribune***, October 12, 1963.

[11] Teresa's engagement at the Met endured from 1973 to 1992.

[12] ***Greenwich Village News Magazine***, March-April, 1977, 16-19.

[13] See Claude Marks, ***World Artists 1980-1990.*** New York: H.W. Wilson, 1991, 268.

[14] Eunice Agar, "Richard Miller," ***American Artist***, 52:546 (January 1988) 52-55, 85-86.

[15] Theodore F. Wolff, "Why Painting is Worth the Risks," ***The Christian Science Monitor***, June 19, 1990, 12.

Catalogue of the Exhibition

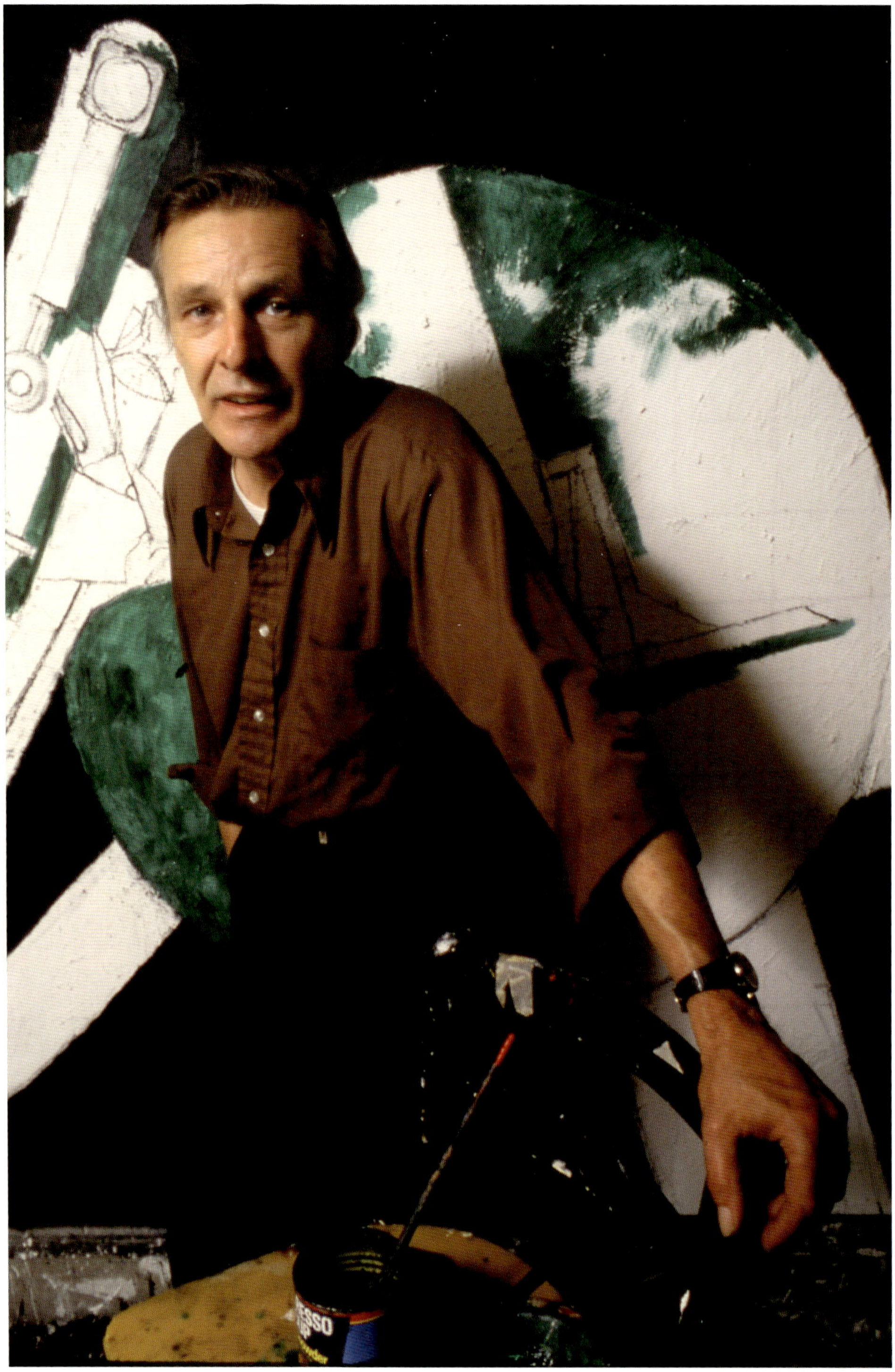

Richard Kidwell Miller, ca. 1990. Photo by William Goidell.

Artist's Statement

I draw constantly. Although my paintings are composites of many drawings, the sense of risk, of spontaneous discovery, is essential. When the conclusions become predictable, I know I must change. Because of this, throughout my life as a painter, my art has undergone many changes. In this way, the act of painting is continually exciting and unpredictable, each change a rebirth. Yet curiously, continuity prevails, in the profound sense, one never really changes. One's commitment to self and sensibility remains constant.

1.

Counterpoint
Gouache & collage on wood
10.5 x 10 inches
1964

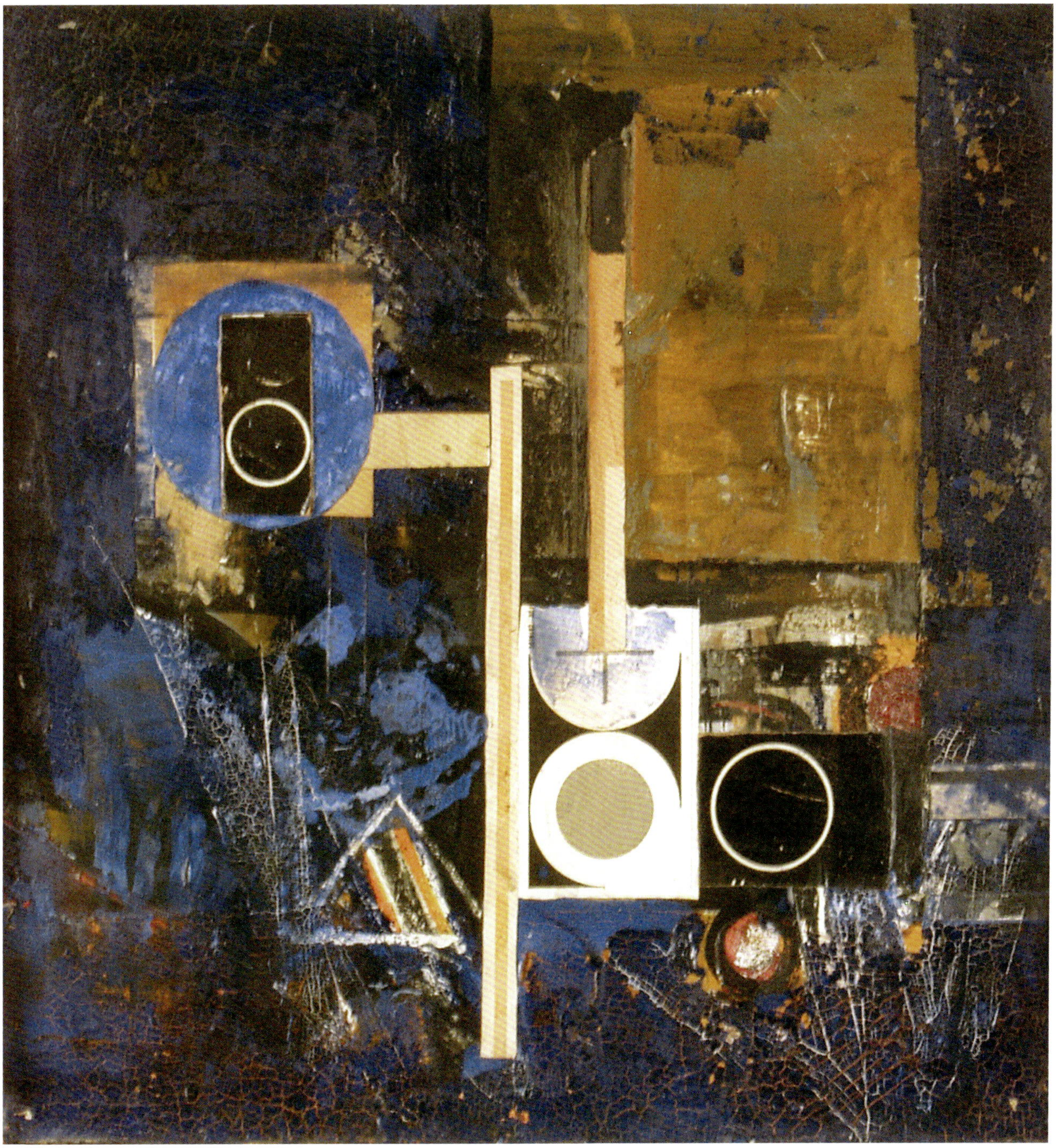

2.

Square Minus One
Gouache and collage on wood
12 x 13 inches
1964

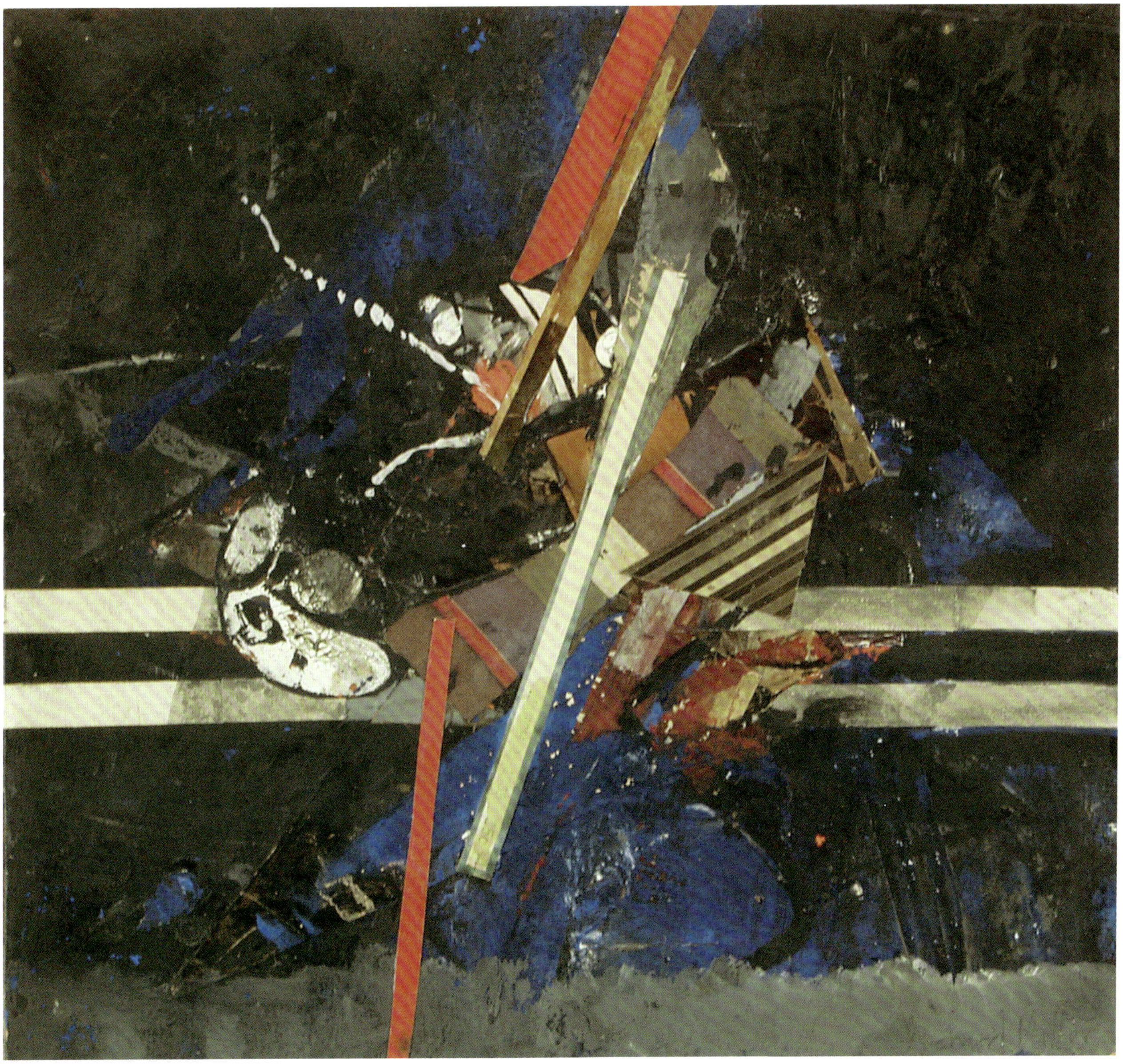

3.

Collision Course
Oil & wood on canvas
26 x 26.5 inches
1969
West Virginia Historical Art Collection
West Virginia University

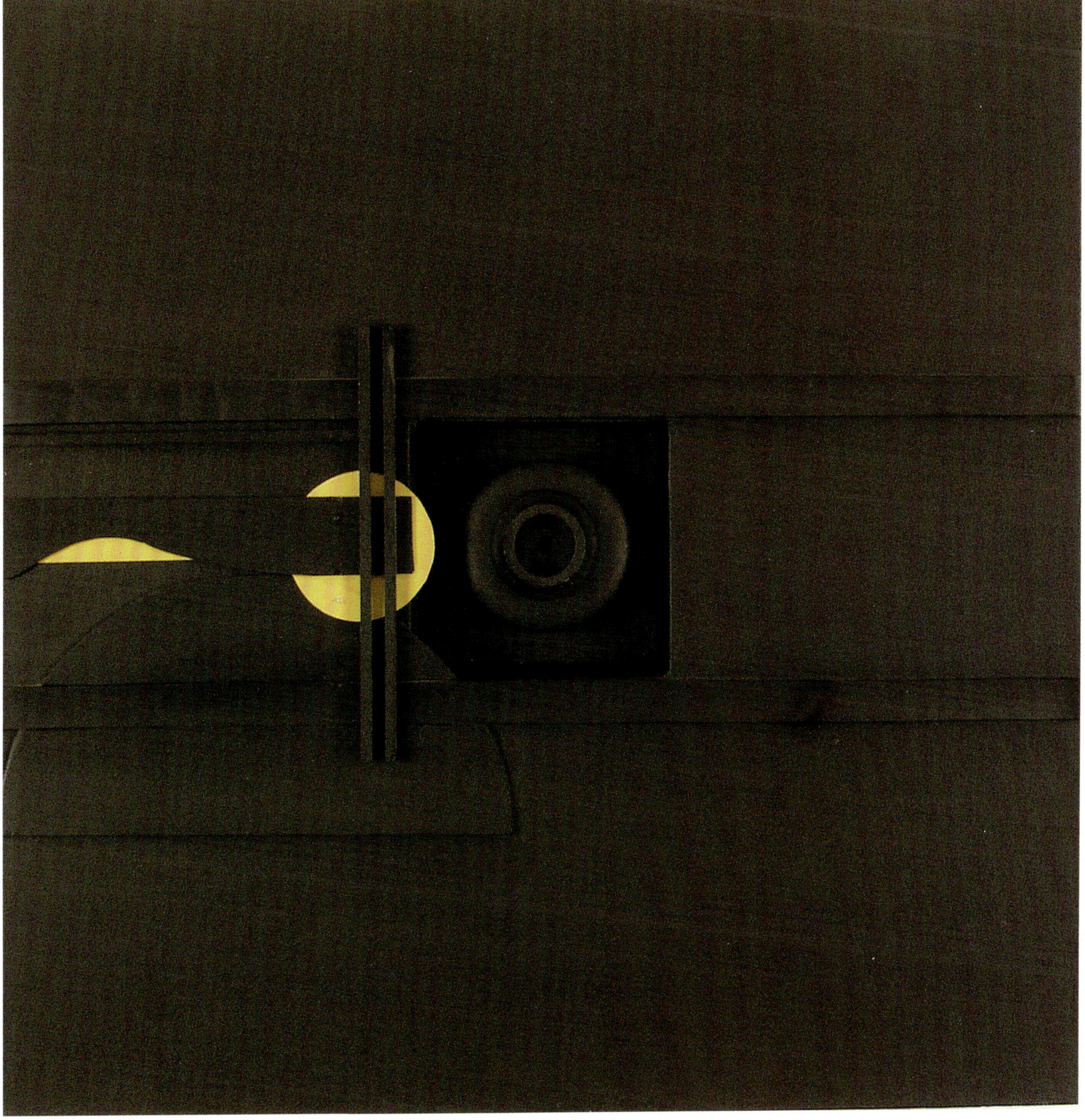

4.

Juggernaut
Acrylic & wood construction on canvas
25 x 25 inches
1972

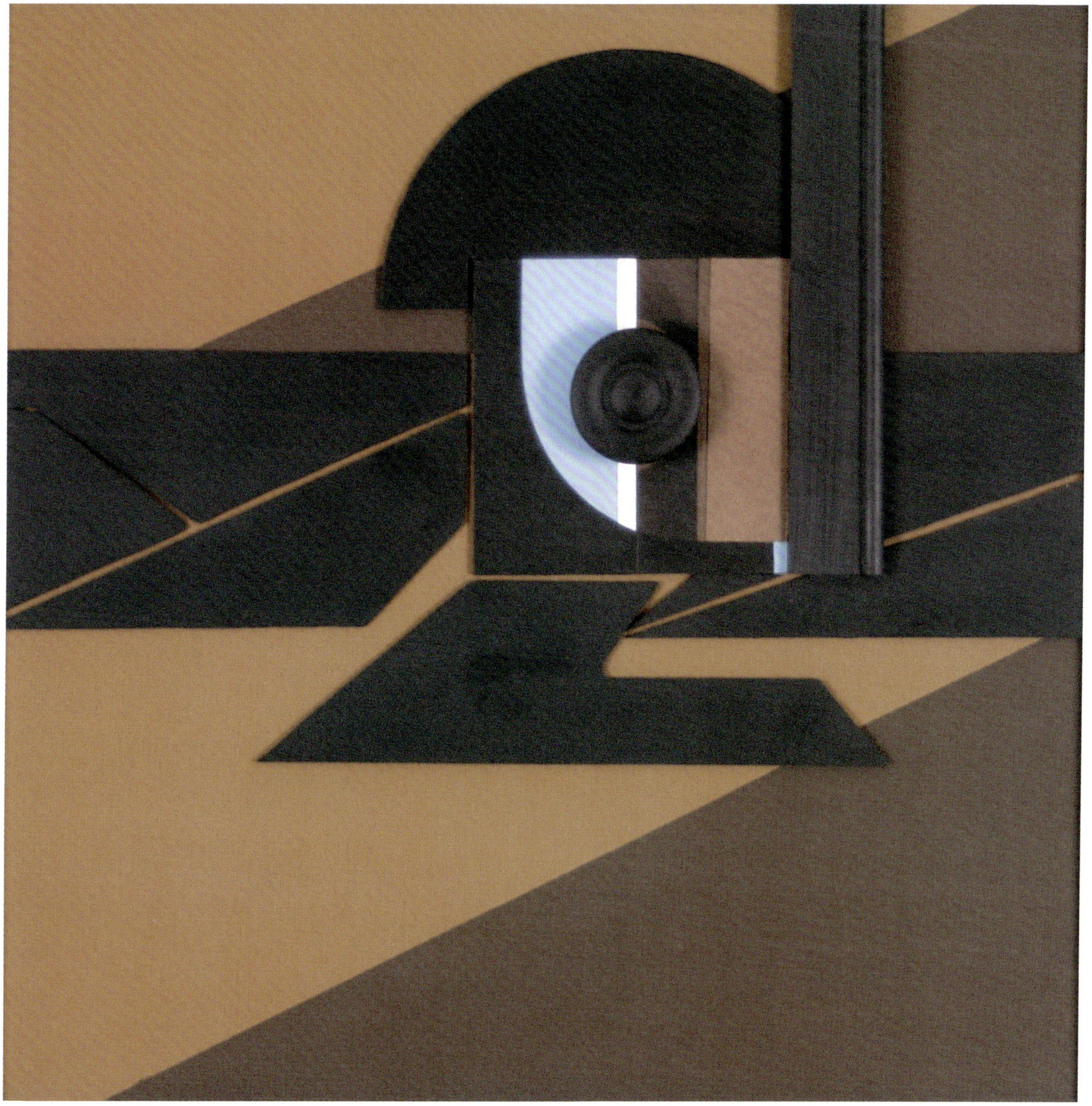

5.

Cinq Bleu
Acrylic & wood construction on canvas
26 x 26 inches
1973

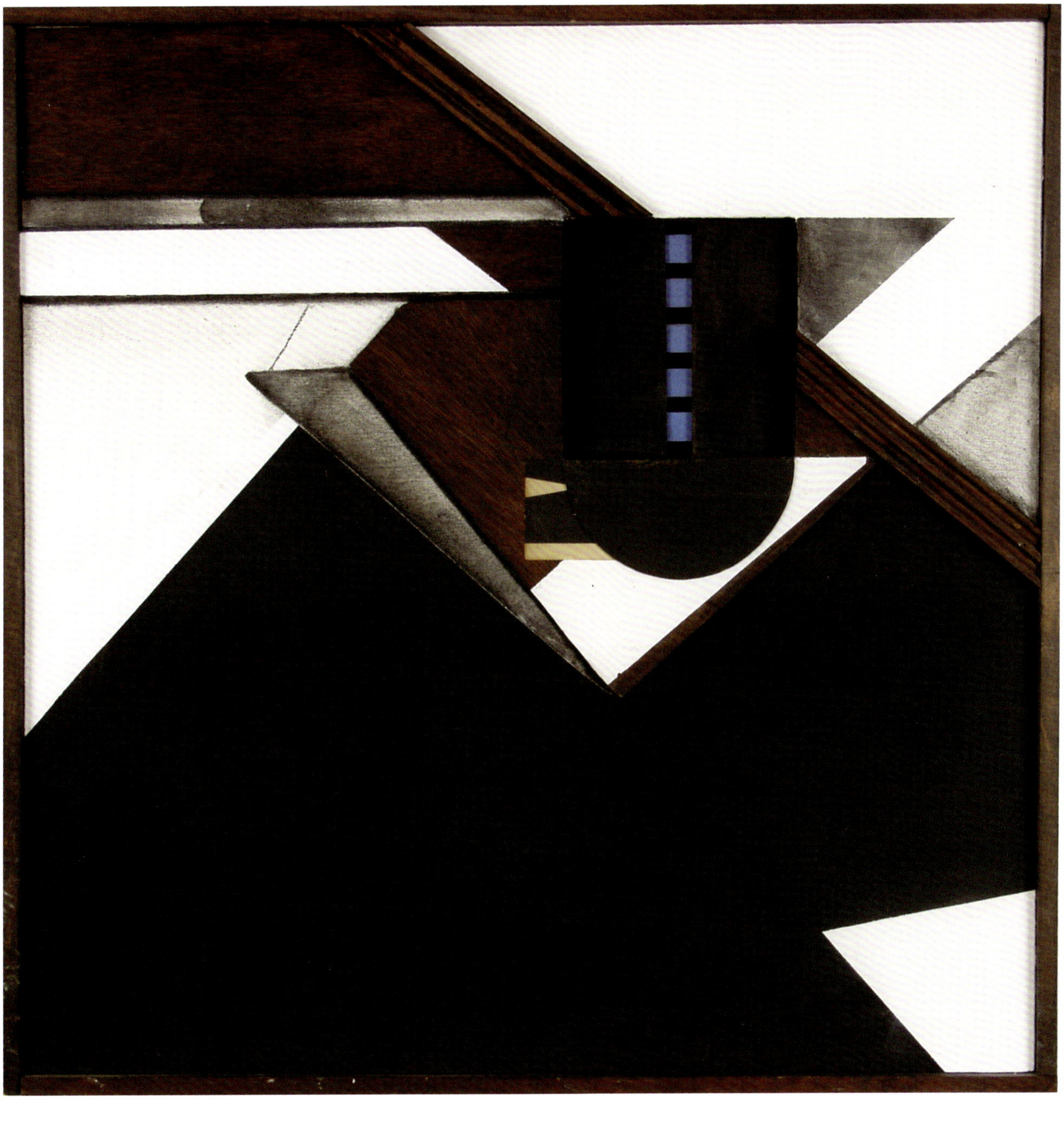

6.

Red Hiding
Oil & collage on canvas
18 x 24 inches
1976

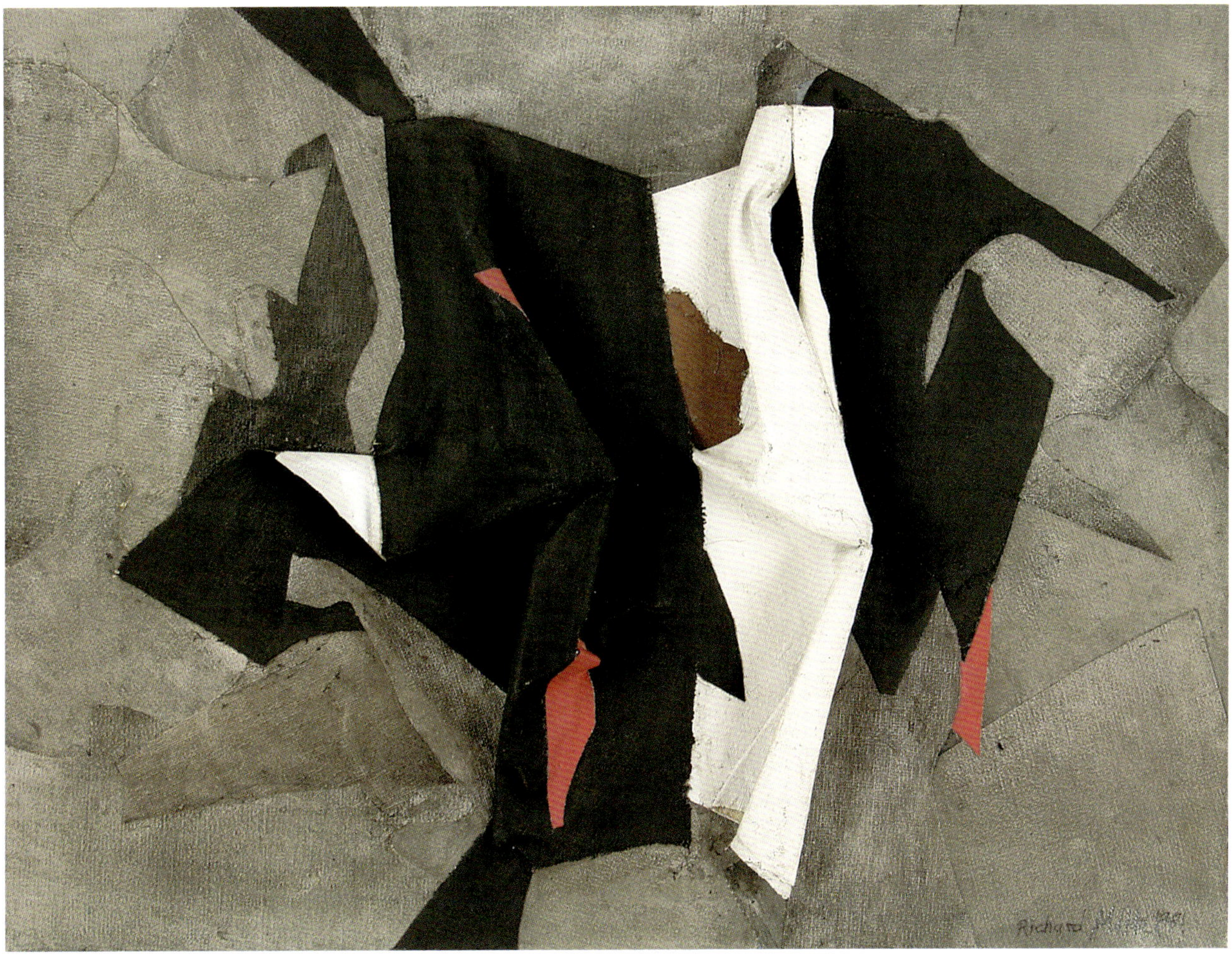

7.

Dark Intrusion
Acrylic & canvas collage on canvas
18 x 24 inches
1980

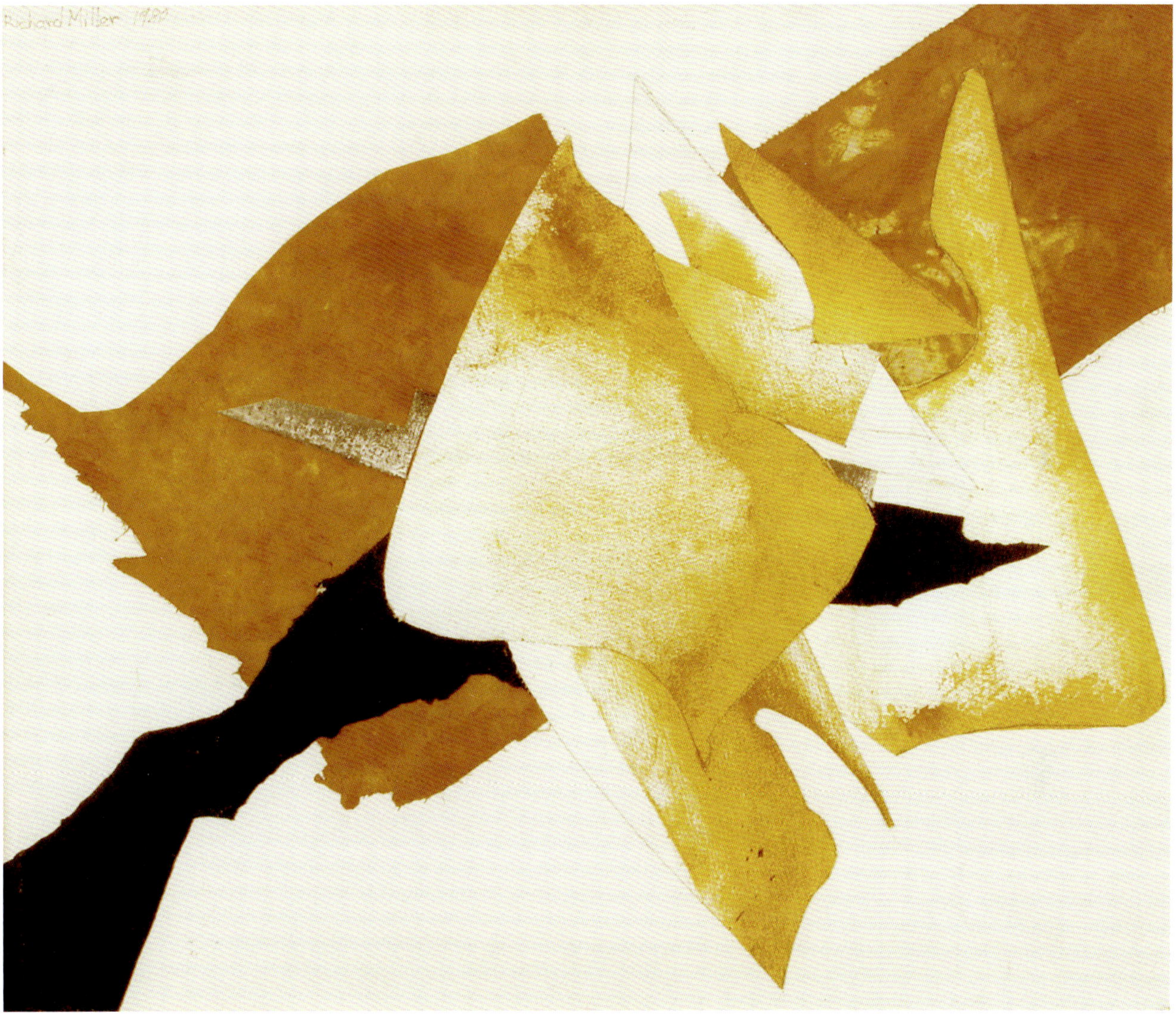

8.

Form in a Landscape II
Acrylic & folded canvas on canvas
16 x 18 inches
1982

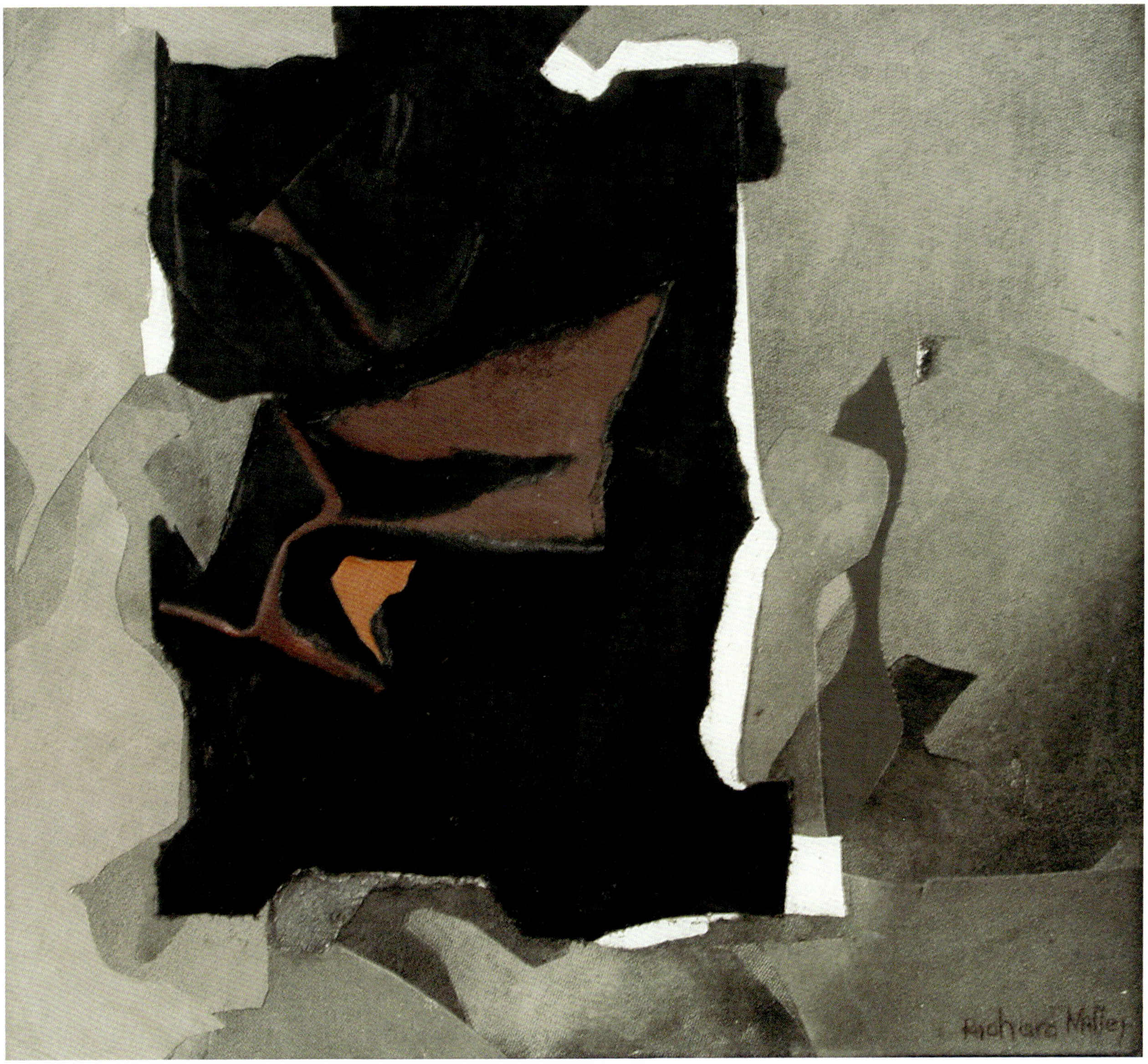
Richard Miller

9.

Labyrinth
Acrylic & folded canvas on canvas
20.5 x 11 inches
1982

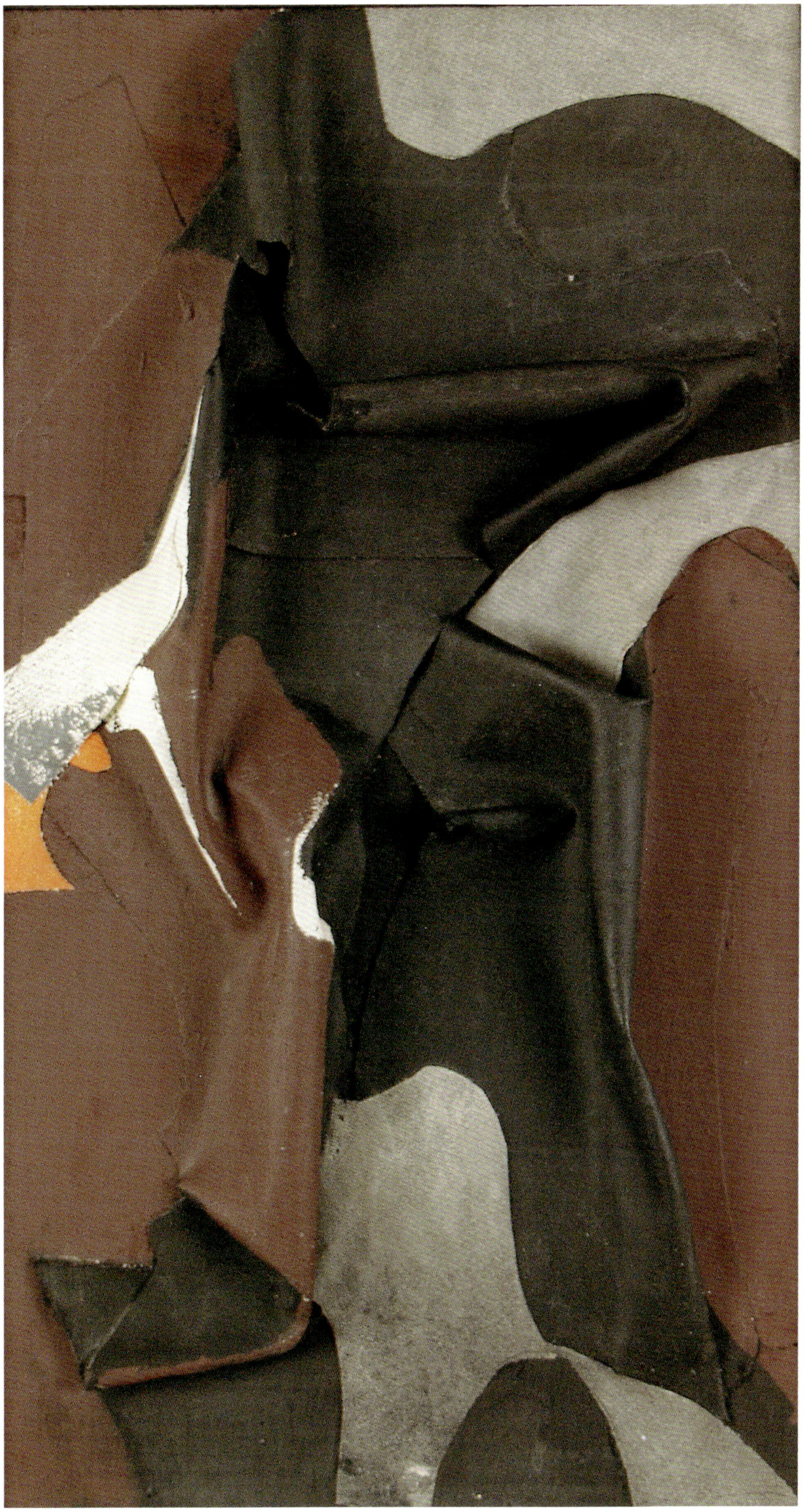

10.

Specter II
Acrylic & folded canvas on canvas
18 x 29 inches
1982

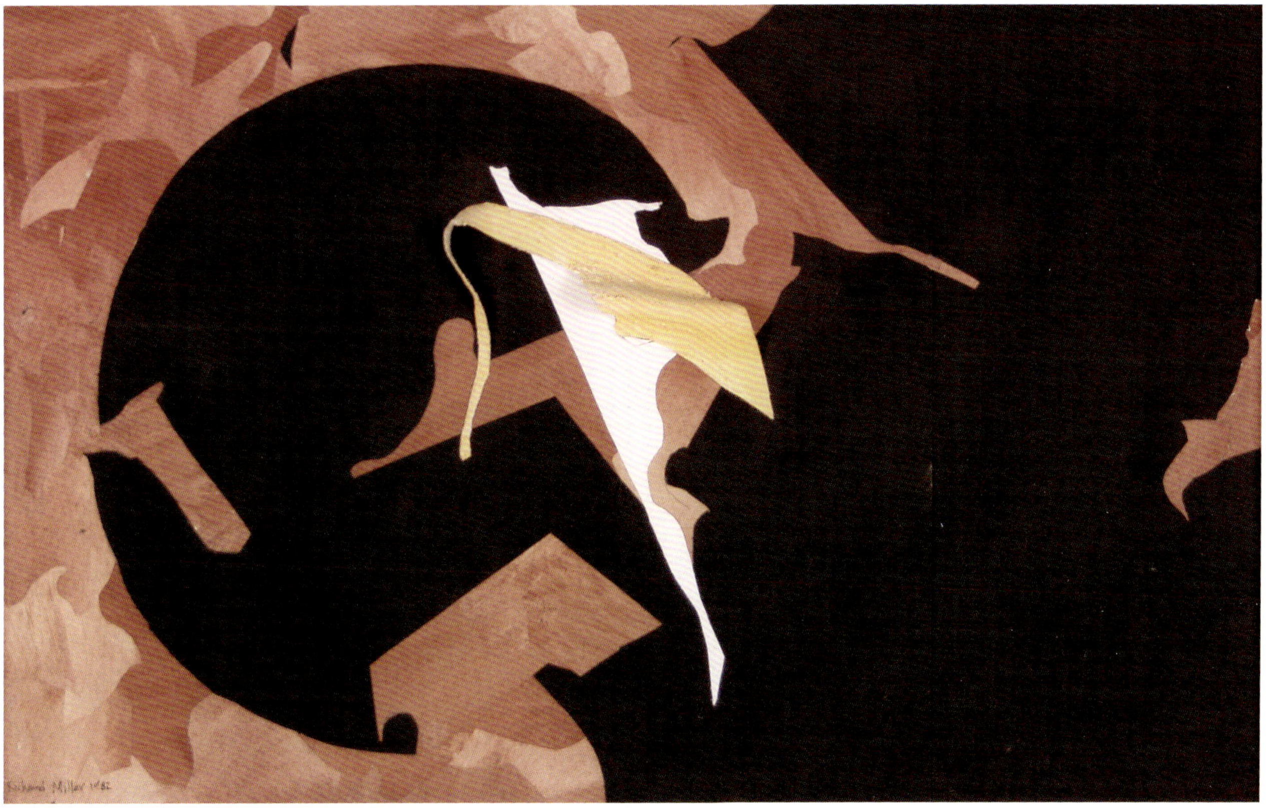

11.

White Passage
Acrylic & canvas collage on canvas
19 x 24 inches
1983

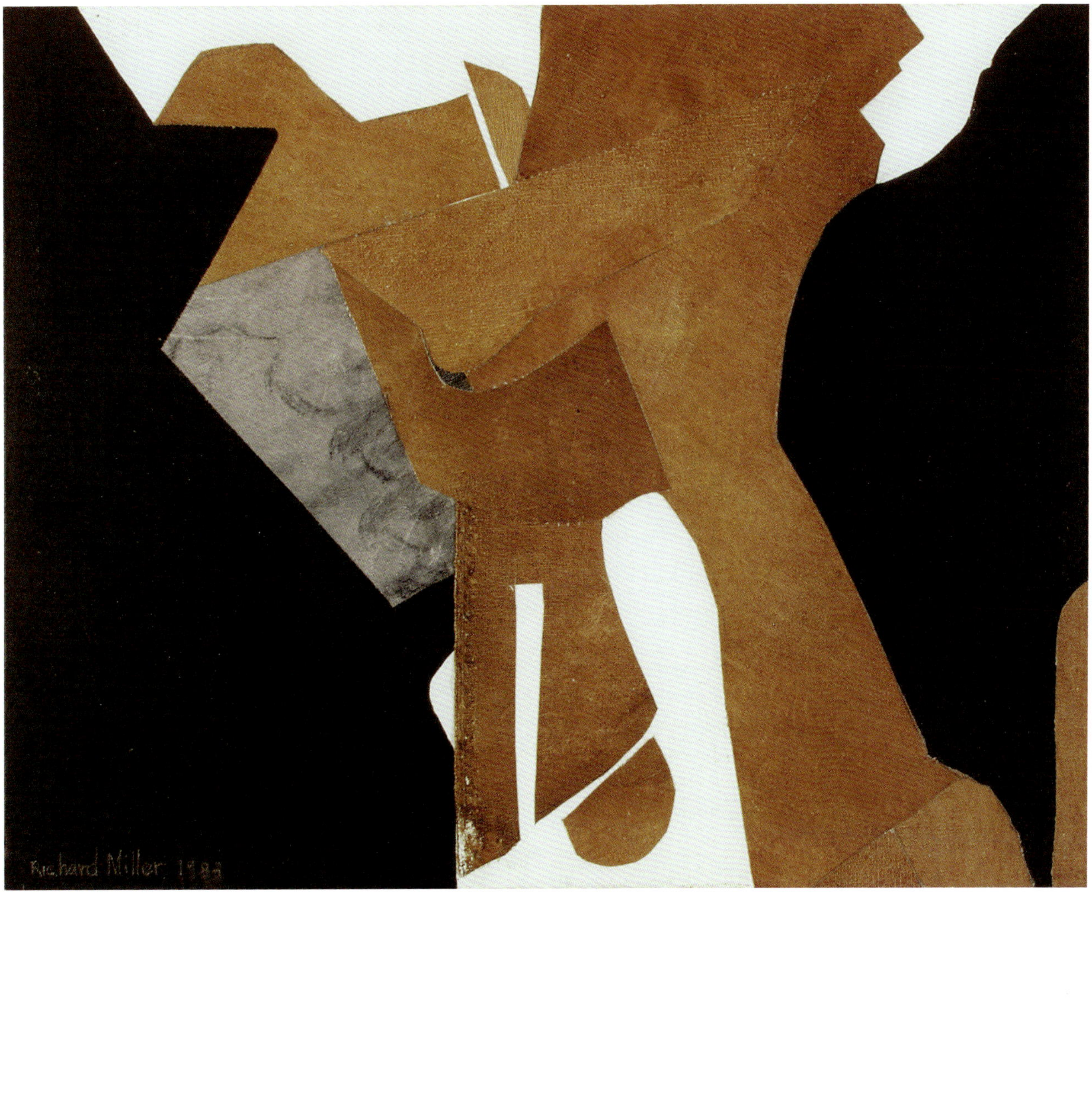

12.

Blue Twice
Acrylic & canvas collage on canvas
24 x 18 inches
1984

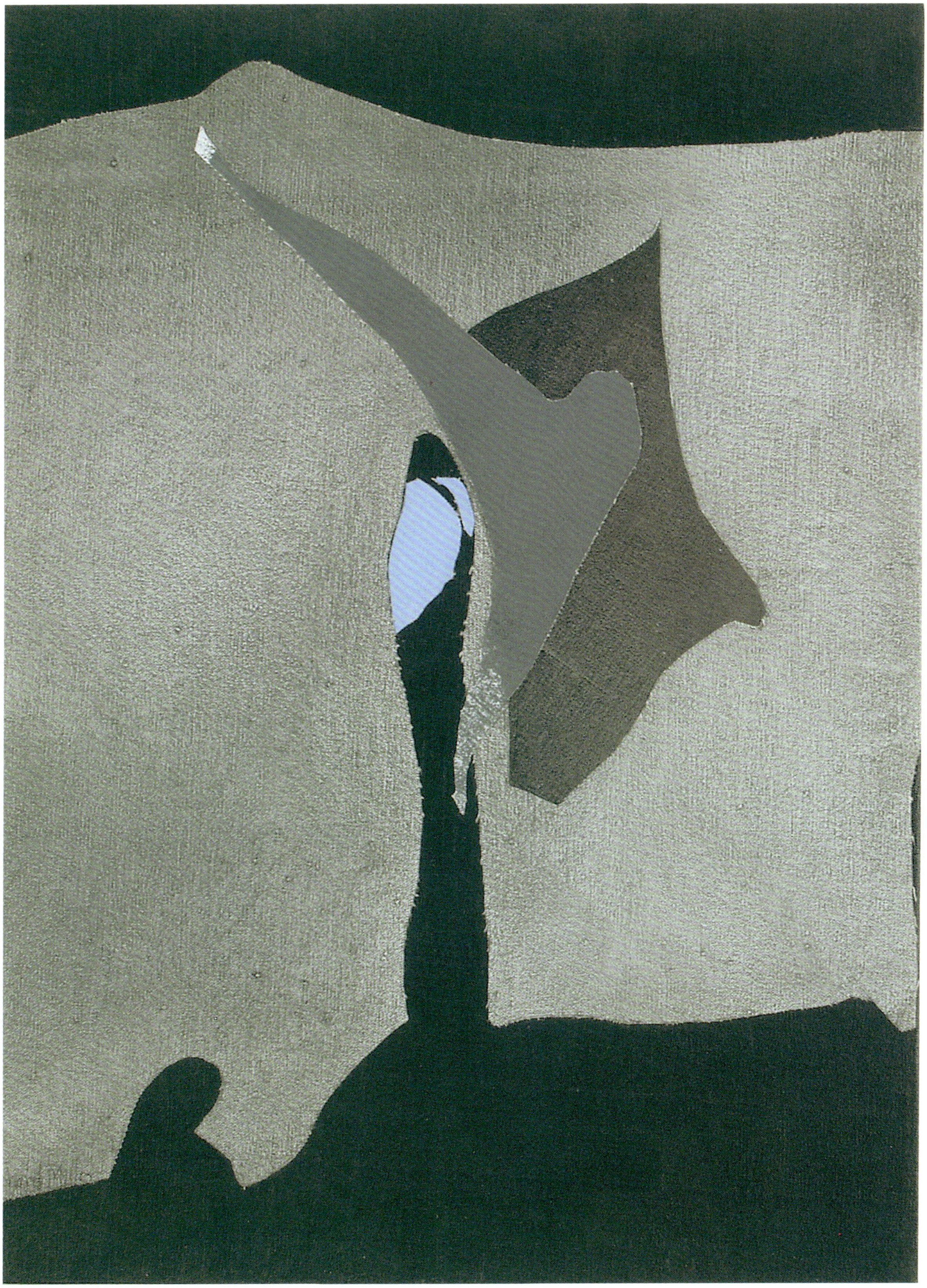

13.

Glass and Grape
Acrylic, oil & oil stick on canvas
45 x 45 inches
1986
West Virginia Historical Art Collection
West Virginia University

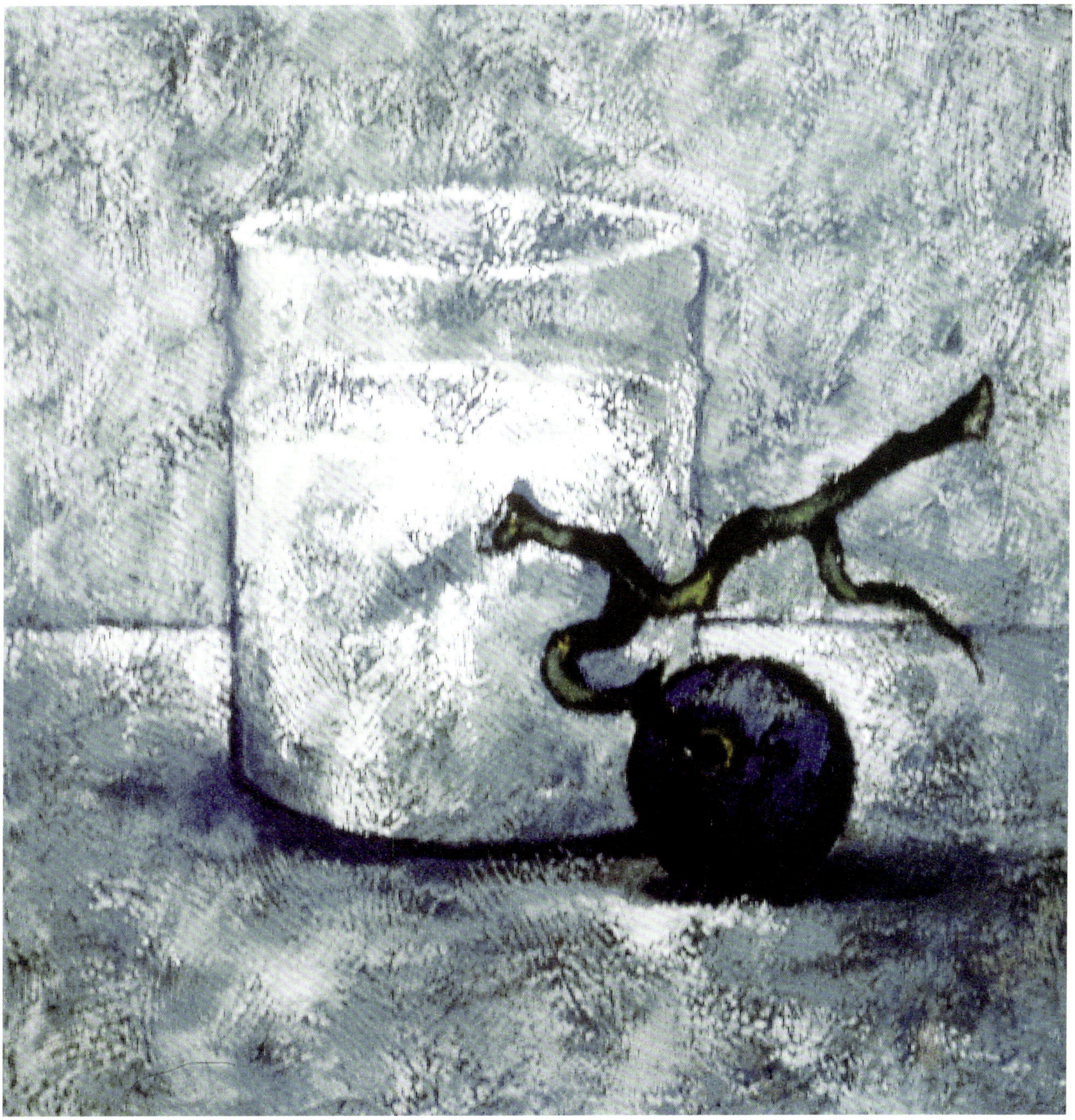

14.

The Red Fork
Acrylic, oil & oil stick on canvas
36 x 36 inches
1987

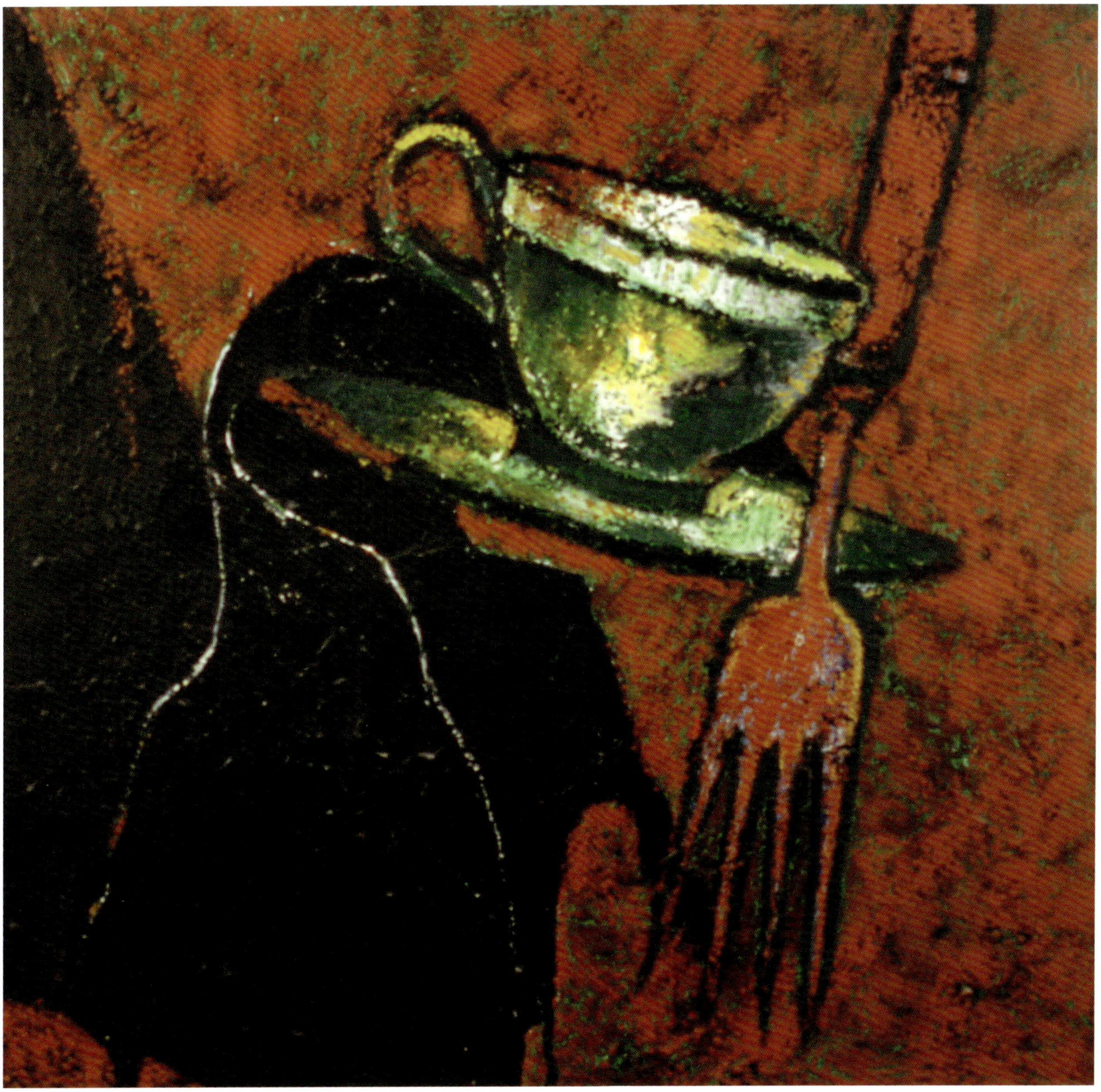

15.

The Return
Oil and oil stick on canvas
37 x 20 inches
1989

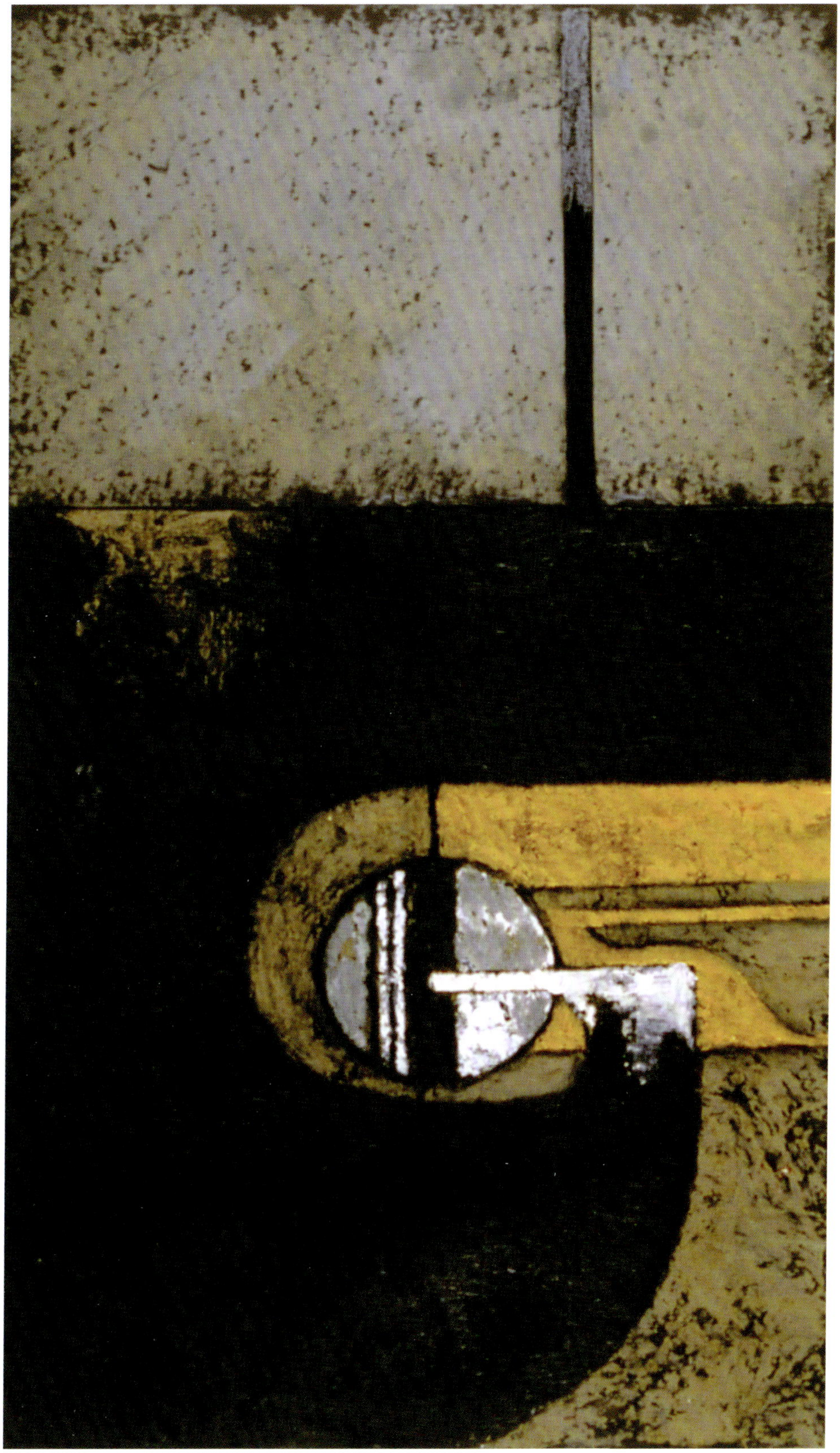

16.

The Trove
Oil, oil stick & collage on canvas
24 x 34 inches
1990

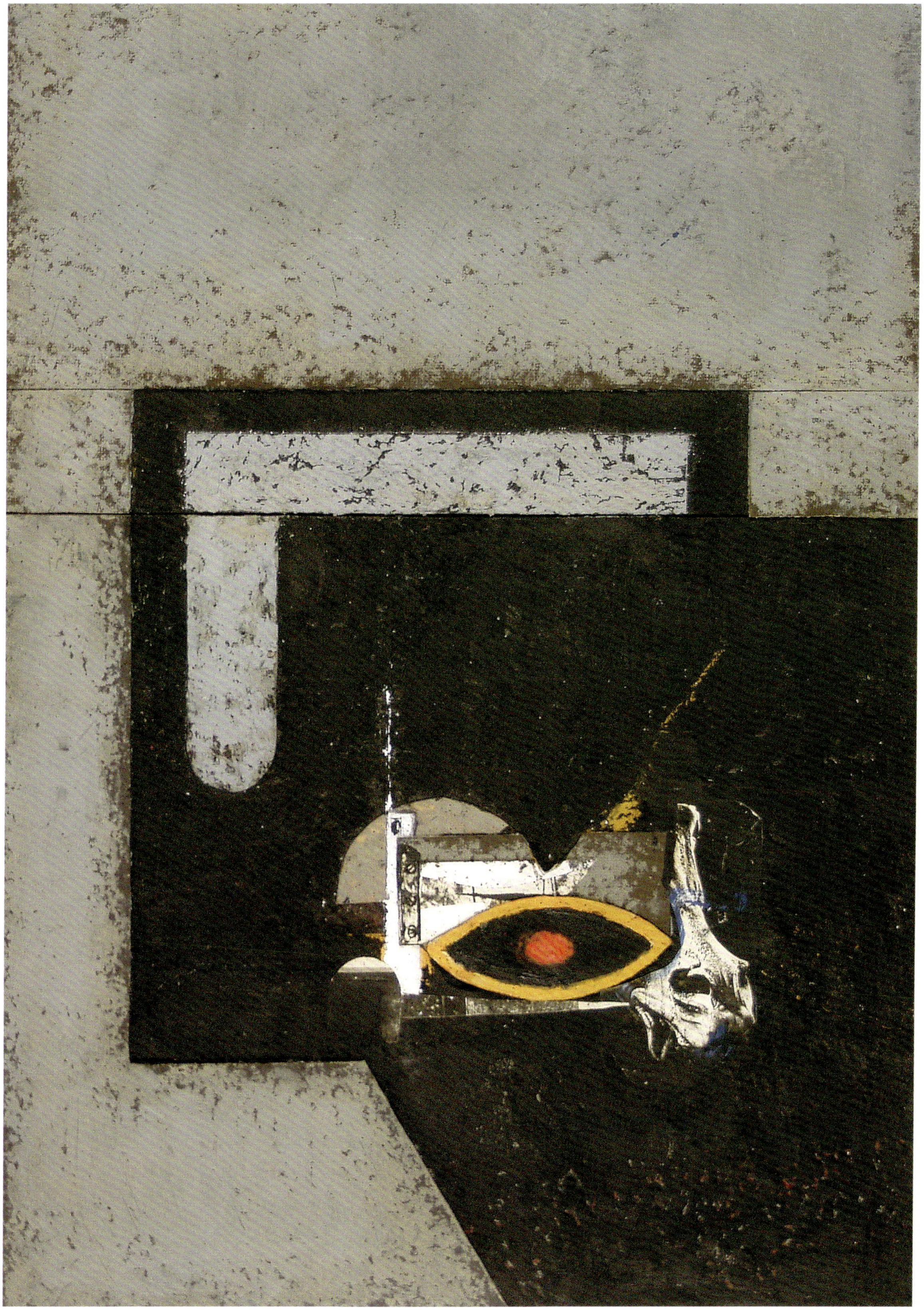

17.

Table Form
Oil stick & collage on canvas
30 x 30 inches
1992

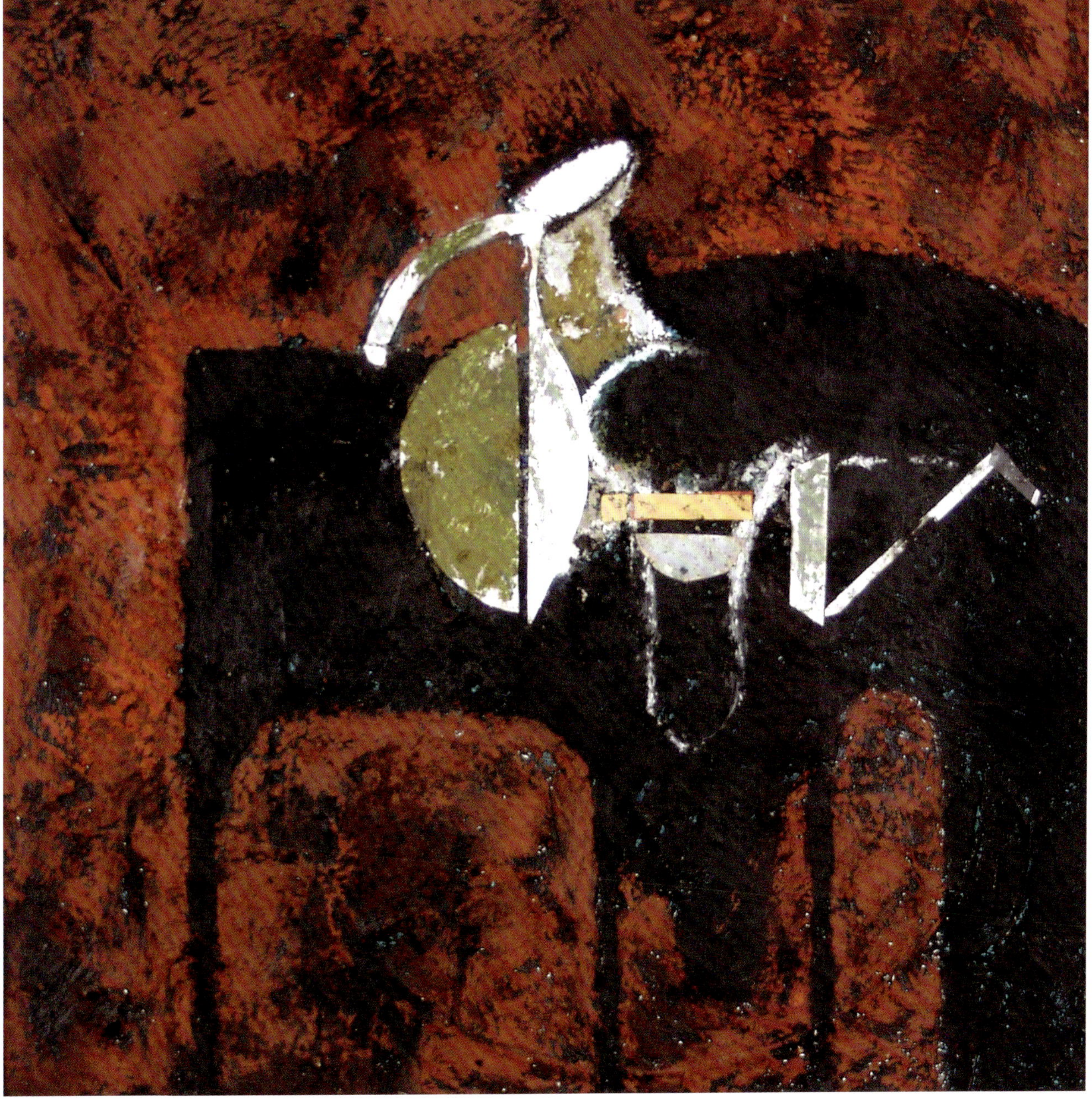

18.

Black Bar Form
Acrylic & collage on canvas
23 x 17 inches
1994

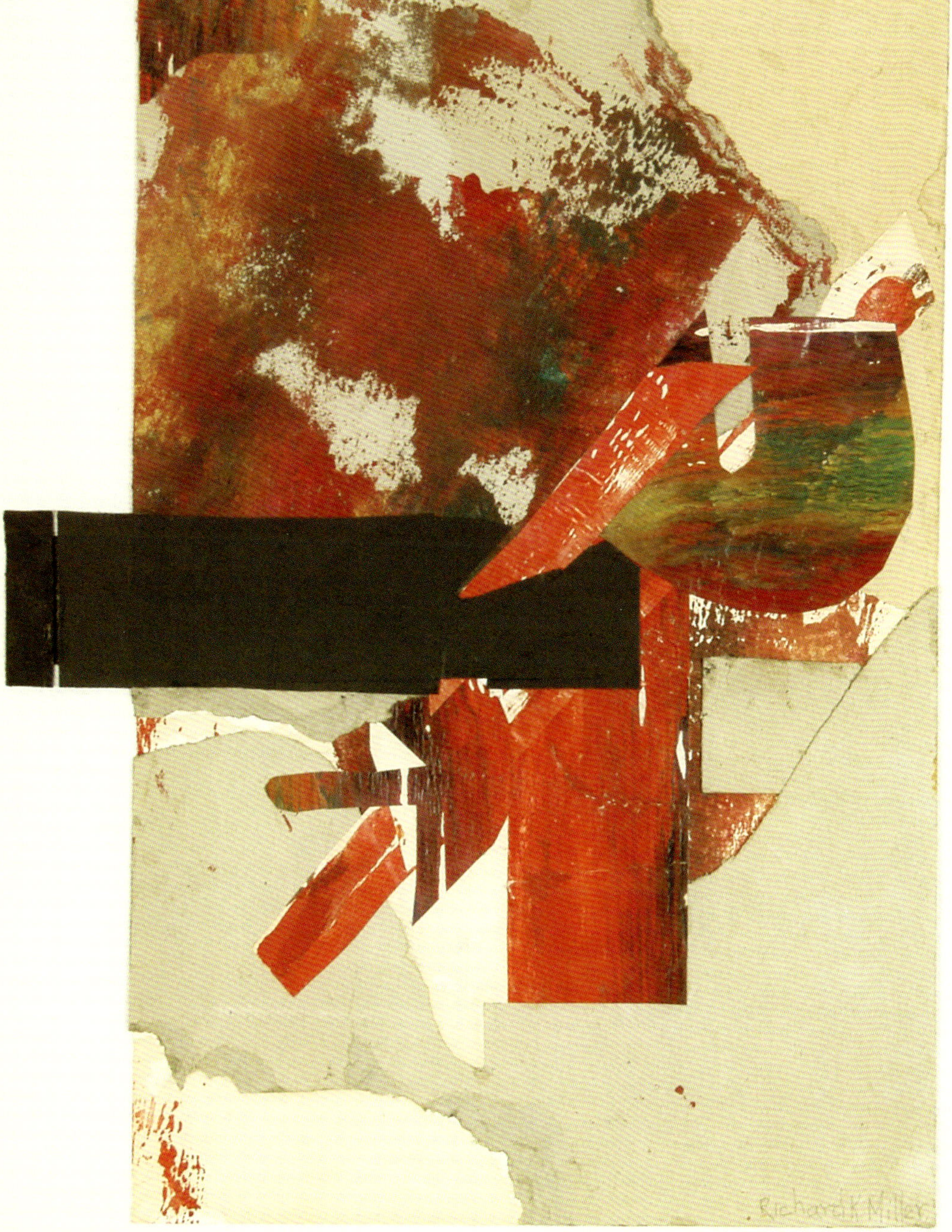

19.

The Signal
Oil, oil stick & collage on canvas
24 x 20 inches
1998

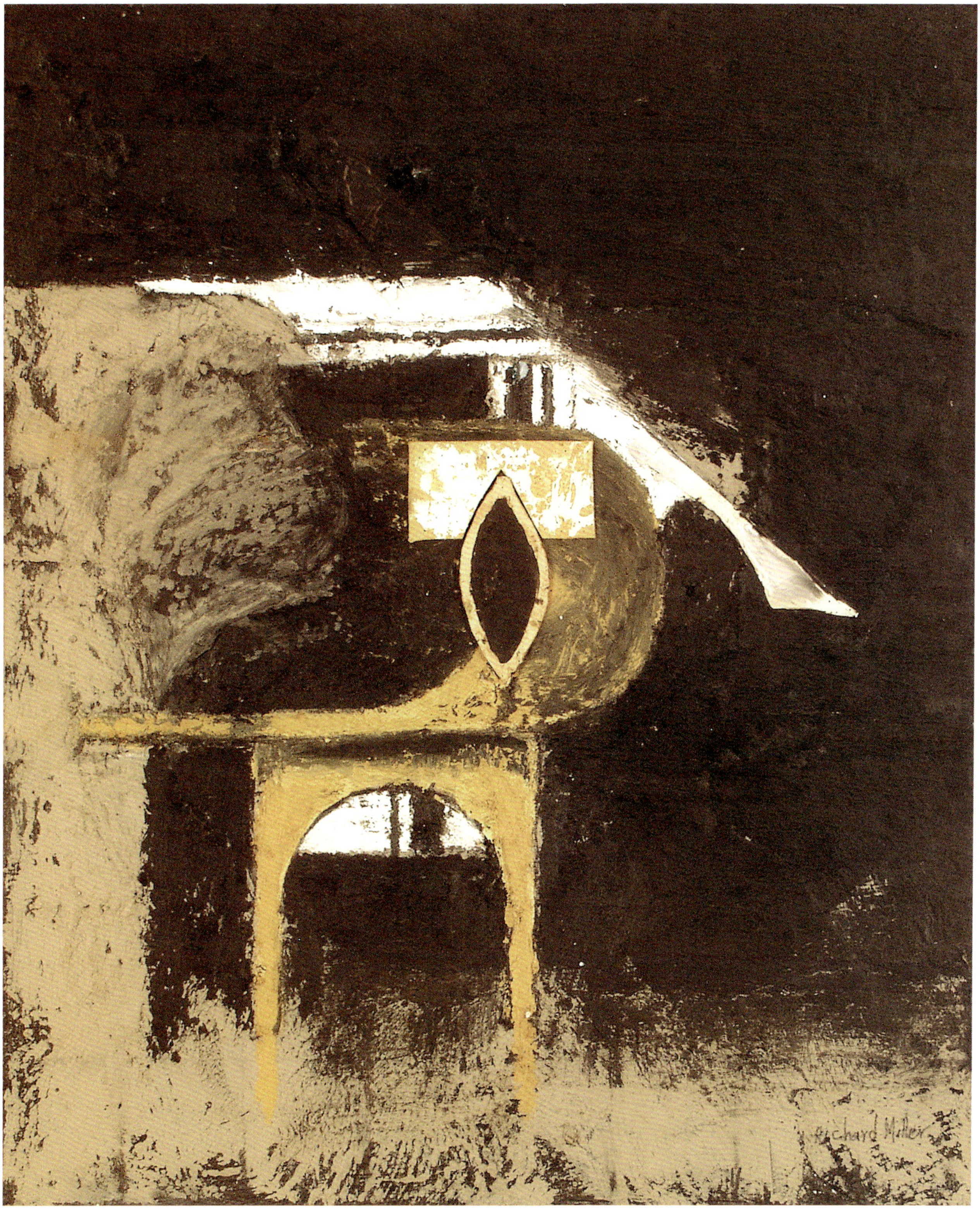
Richard Miller

20.

Standing Form
Oil, oil stick & collage on canvas
80 x 56 inches
1998

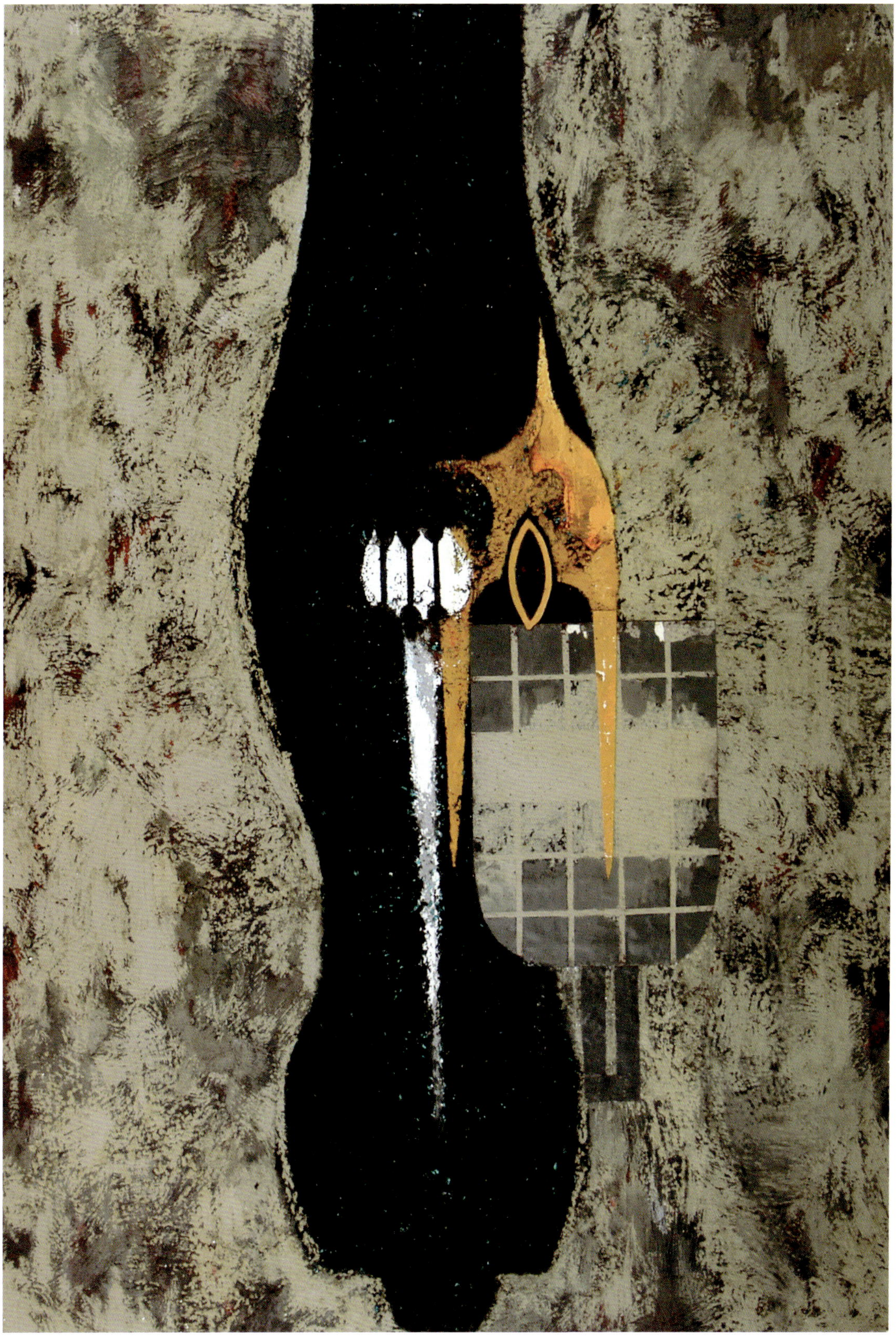

21.

Yellow Jack II
Oil, oil stick & collage on canvas
47 x 44 inches
1999
West Virginia Historical Art Collection
West Virginia University

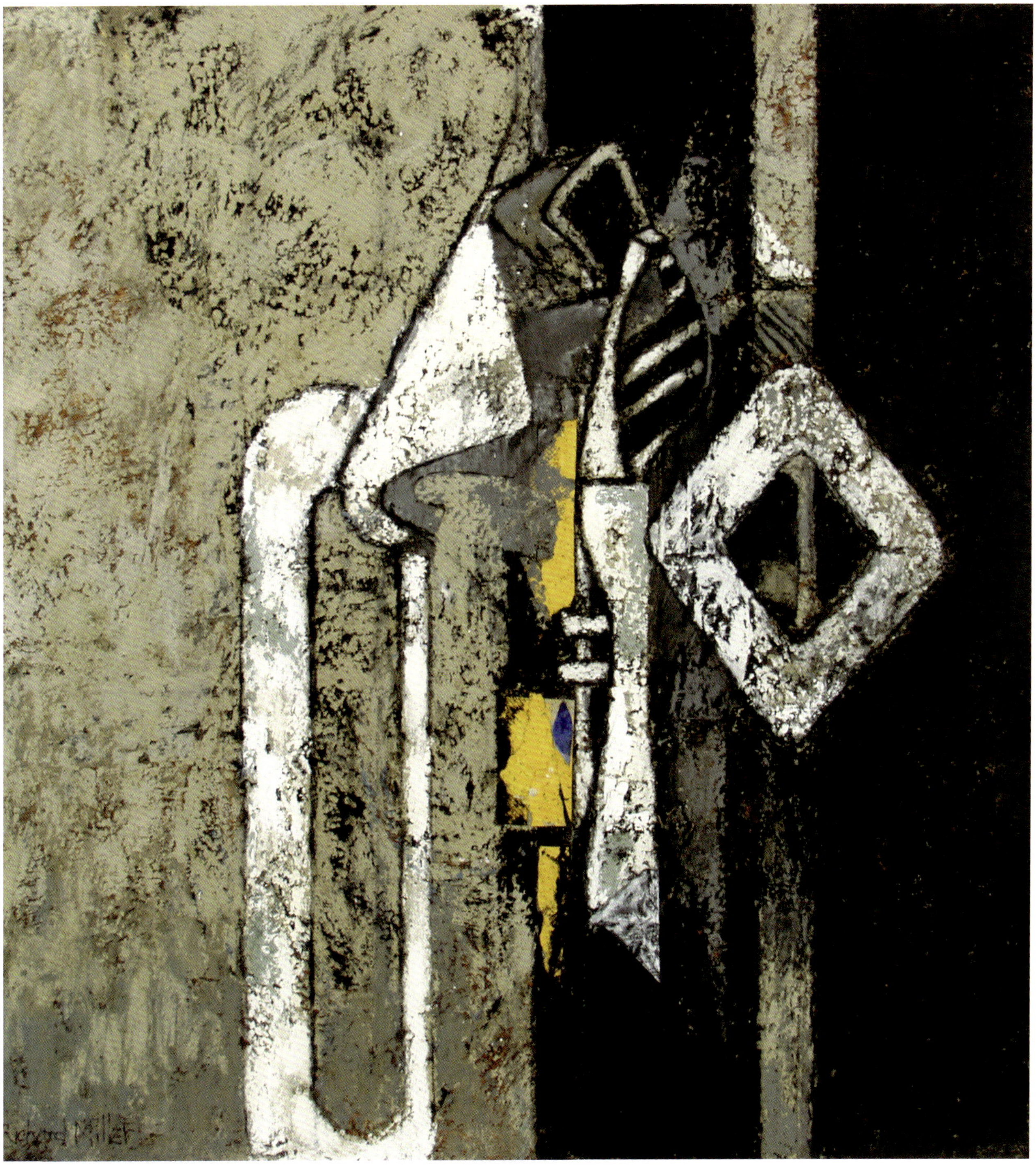

22.

Red Treasure
Oil, oil stick & collage on canvas
54 x 36 inches
2000

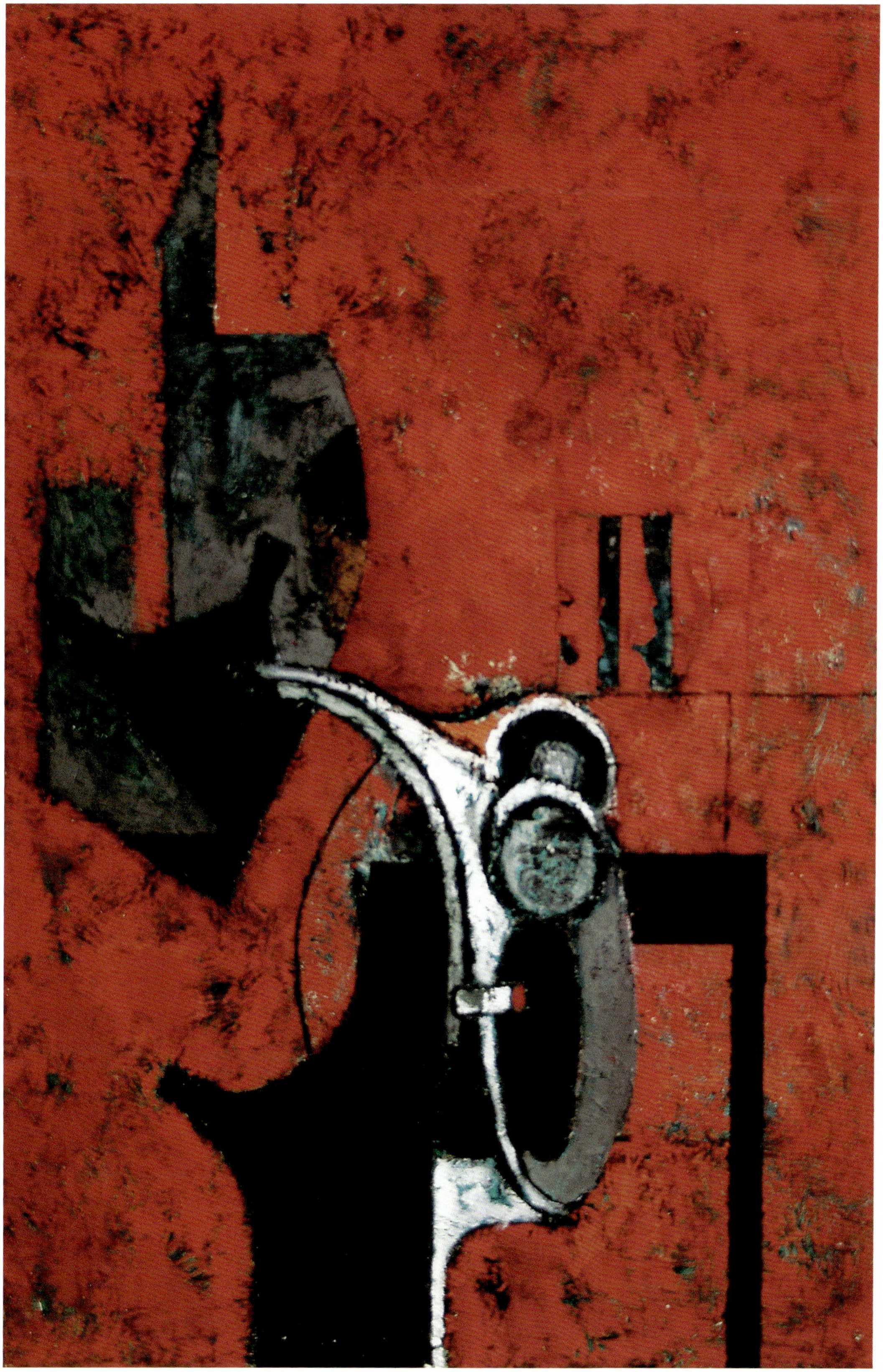

23.

Study for a Monument
Oil, oil stick & collage on canvas
50 x 32 inches
2001

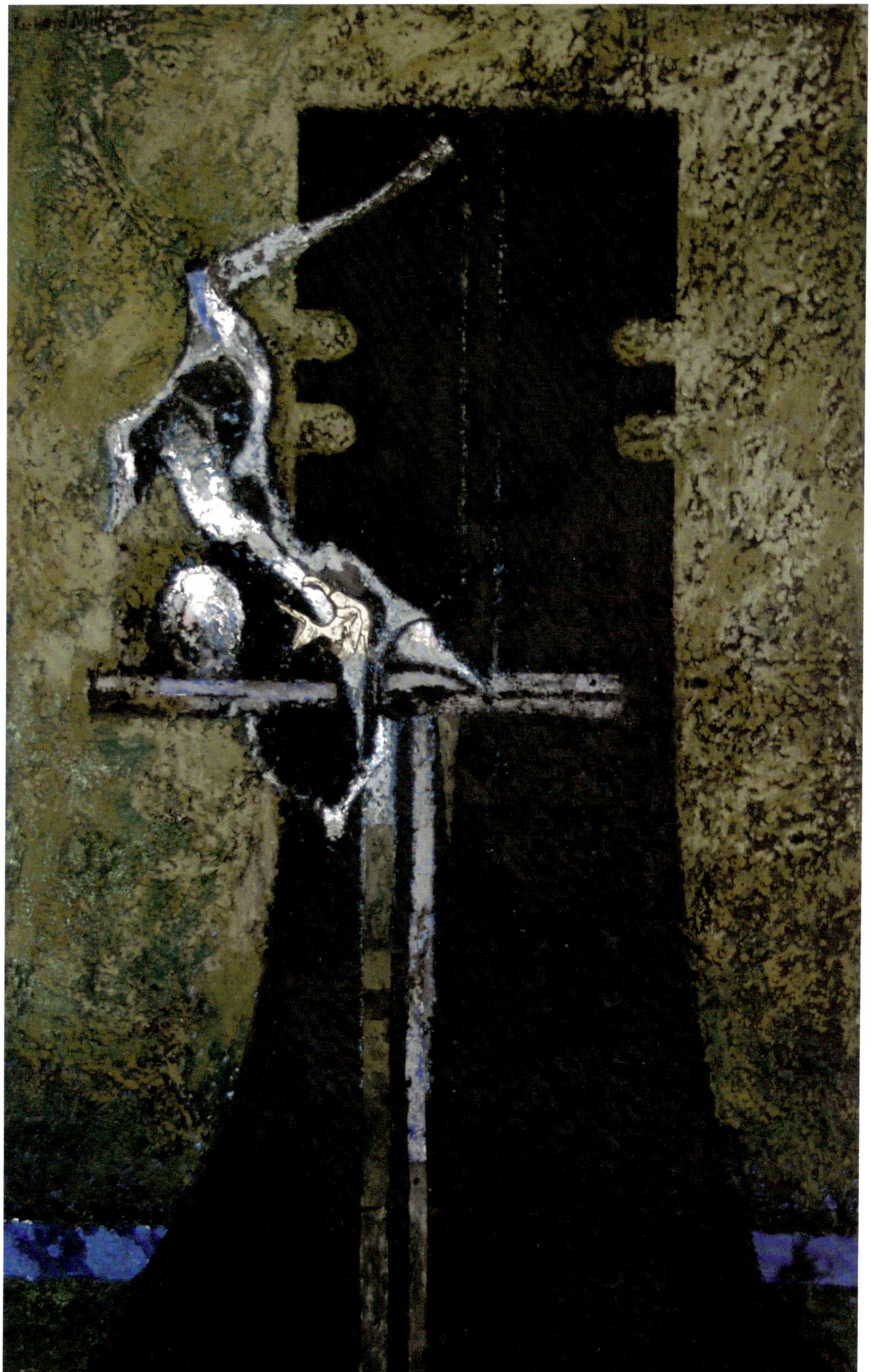

24.

The Second Source
Oil & oil stick on canvas
80 x 56 inches
2001

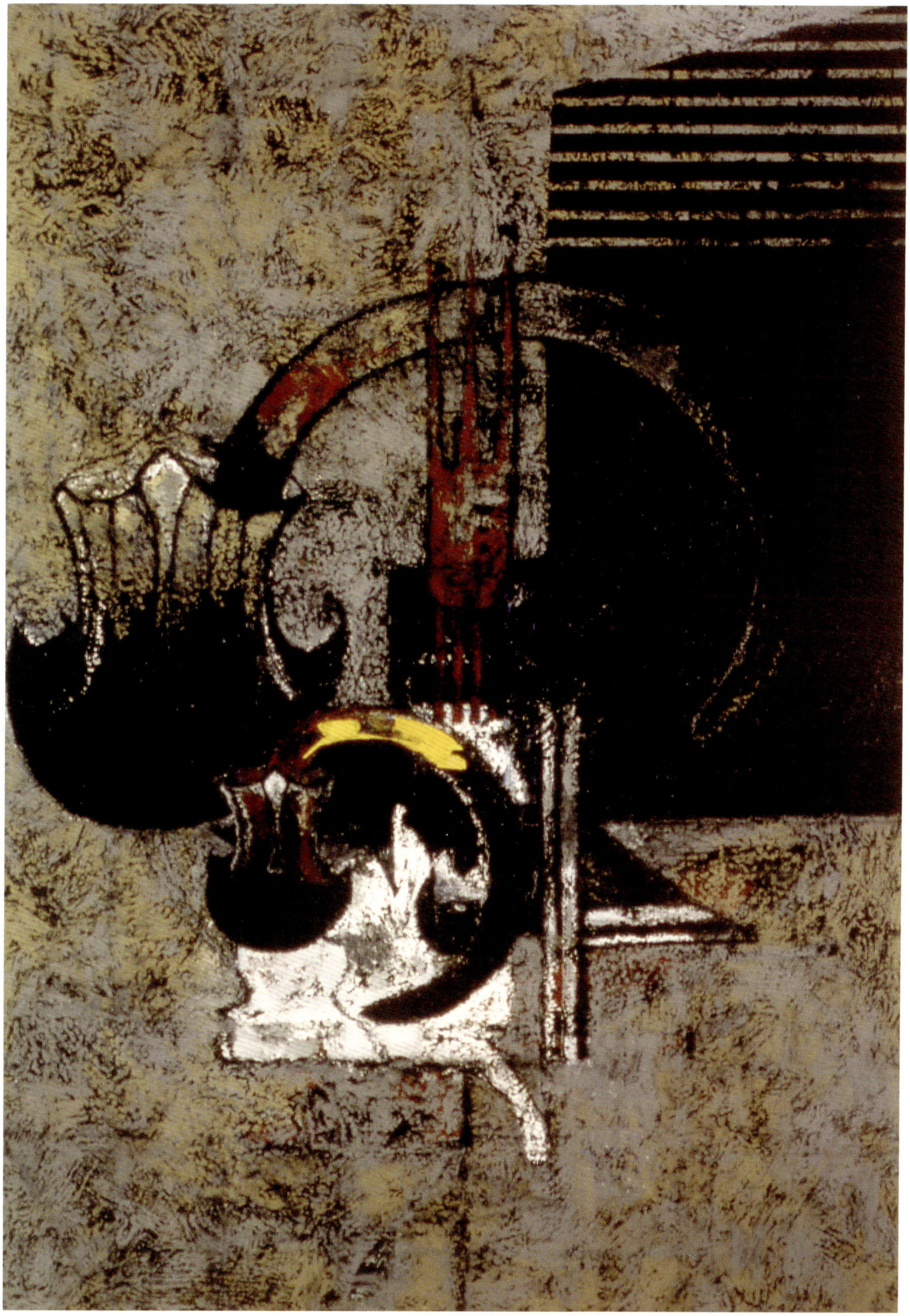

25.

Ancient Image
Acrylic, linoleum & oil stick on canvas
25 x 20 inches
2003

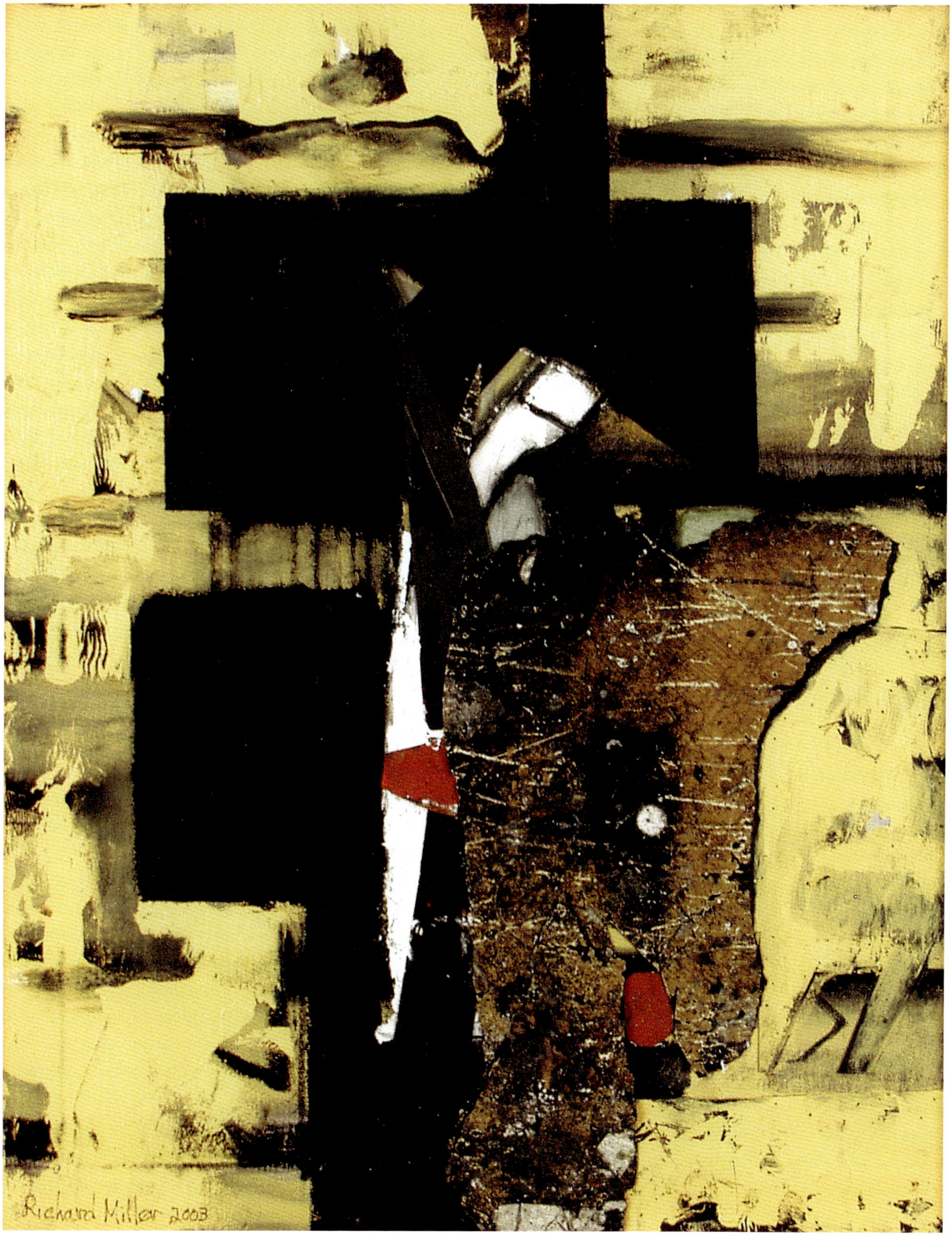
Richard Miller 2003

Richard Kidwell Miller

Selected Exhibitions:

Group Exhibitions:

2002 – "Art of the Northeast," Silvermine Guild Arts Center, New Canaan, CT
1996 – "171st Annual Exhibition," National Academy of Design, New York City, NY
1996 – "Art of the Northeast," Silvermine Guild Arts Center, New Canaan, CT
1995 – Noel Gallery, New Rochelle, NY
1993 – "Recent Acquisitions," Watkins Gallery, Washington, DC
1988 – Glass Art Gallery, N.Y.C. 1994,1995, 1996
1987 – Guest Exhibition, Viridian Gallery, New York City, NY
1986 – Levitan Gallery, New York City, NY
1985 – "On the Line: An Exhibition of Contemporary Drawing," Hastings-on-Hudson Museum Annual, NY
1984 – "Twelve Artists," Noel Gallery, New Rochelle, NY
1983 – "Beyond the Wall," Aaron Berman Gallery, New York City, NY
1981 – "Ambience/Stimuli," Alternative Museum, New York City, NY
1980 – 31st New England Exhibition of Painting and Sculpture (Shoemaker Award for Painting, Juror: Henry Geldzahler)
1980 – American Drawings III, Portsmouth, VA
1980 – 13th National Print Exhibition, Silvermine Guild, CT
1978 – 12th National Print Exhibition, Silvermine Guild, CT
1974 – "Mainstream 74," Marietta College, Marietta, OH
1973 – New Images, Martha Jackson Gallery, New York City, NY
1967 – Tokyo International, Tokyo, Japan
1965 – 11th Annual Drawing & Sculpture Exhibition, Ball State University, Muncie, IN
1965 – "Art in Process," Finch College Museum, New York City, NY
1965 – American Federation of Art (Tour of "Art in Process")
1964 – Pennsylvania Academy of Fine Arts Annual, Philadelphia, PA
1962 – Chicago Art Institute Annual, Chicago, IL

1962 – Museum of Modern Art Lending Library, New York City, NY
1961 – Carnegie International, Pittsburgh, PA
1960 – Nebraska Art Association Annual, University of Nebraska Art Galleries, Lincoln, NB
1958 – "Fulbright Painters at the Whitney," Whitney Museum, New York City, NY (This exhibit toured 19 additional sites across United States)
1957 – Provincetown Arts Festival, Provincetown, MA
1956 – "Whitney Annual," Whitney Museum, New York City, NY
1954 – Salon de National, Paris, France
1953 – Corcoran Gallery of Art, Washington, DC (First Prize for Still Life Painting)
1951 – Pennsylvania Academy of Fine Arts Annual, Philadelphia, PA
1951 – Corcoran Gallery of Art, Washington, DC
1951 – Smithsonian Institution, Washington, DC (First Prize for Figure Painting)
1948 – Phillips Collection, Artists of Washington & Baltimore, Washington, DC

Solo Exhibitions:

2004 – West Virginia University, Morgantown, WV
2001 – Jewish Community Center of Mid-Westchester, NY
2000 – John Jay Gallery, New York City, NY
1995 – John Jay Gallery, New York City, NY
1989 – Westchester Gallery, White Plains, NY
1983 – Aaron Berman Gallery, New York City, NY
1982 – Westbeth Gallery, New York City, NY
1976 – Long Island University, Brooklyn, NY
1969 – Jewish Community Center Gallery, Kansas City, MO
1969 – Albrecht Kemper Museum of Art, St. Joseph, MO
1967 – Jefferson Place Gallery, Washington, DC
1966 – Ardas Gallery, Madison, NJ
1965 – Graham Gallery, Ltd., New York City, NY

1962 – Graham Gallery, Ltd., New York City, NY
1960 – Graham Gallery, Ltd., New York City, NY
1955 – Baltimore Museum of Art, Baltimore, MD
1954 – Franz Bader Gallery, Washington, DC
1950 – Trans-Lux Gallery, Washington, DC
1947 – Fairmont State College, Fairmont, WV

Selected Collections:

Watkins Gallery, American University, Washington, DC
Hirschhorn Museum and Sculpture Garden, Washington, DC
The Phillips Collection, Washington, DC
Memorial Art Gallery of the University of Rochester, Rochester, NY
Albrecht Kemper Museum of Art, St. Joseph, MO
University of Arizona Museum of Art, Tucson, AZ
Richard Brown Baker Collection, New York, NY
Plessey Corporation, General Motors Building, New York, NY
Skidmore, Owings and Merrill, New York, NY
Columbia University, New York, NY
United Cerebral Palsy Association, Rye Brook, NY
West Virginia University Art Collection, Morgantown, WV

Awards:

National Society of Arts and Letters, 2003
Fulbright Fellowship Jury, 1996, 1997, 1998
31 New England Exhibition of Painting and Sculpture, Shoemaker Award for Painting, 1980
Gertrude Vanderbilt Whitney Scholarship, 1948-1953; 1955-1956
Fulbright Fellowship, 1953-1954

Corcoran Gallery of Art, Washington, DC, first Prize: still life painting; third prize: painting, 1953

Smithsonian Institution, third prize, figurative painting, 1950

Washington Times Herald Scholarship, 1944, 1945, 1946

Bibliography:

Agar, Eunice. "Richard Miller," ***American Artist,*** 52:546 (January 1988) 52-55, 85-86.

Art in Process. Exhibition catalogue, Finch College Museum of Art, New York: 1965.

Art International, IV, 1961.

Cummings, Paul. ***Dictionary of Contemporary American Artists.*** 6th ed. New York: St. Martin's Press, 1994

Cuthbert, John A. ***Early Art and Artists in West Virginia.*** Morgantown, WV: WVU Press, 2000.

Falk, Peter Hastings. ***Who Was Who in American Art.*** Madison, CT: Soundview Press, 1999.

Frank, Peter. ***RE-DACT: An Anthology of Art Criticism.*** New York: Willis, Locker and Owens, 1984.

Fulbright Painters [at the Whitney]. Exhibition catalogue. New York: Institute of International Education, 1958.

Gruen, John. "The Galleries," ***New York Herald Times,*** October 12, 1963.

Krantz, Les. ***The American Artist, An Illustrated Survey of Leading Contemporary Americans,*** Chicago: Krantz Company Publishers, Inc., 1985.

Marks, Claude. ***World Artists 1980-1990.*** New York: H.W. Wilson, 1991.

Miller, Marcia. "*Painter: Richard Kidwell Miller,"* Master's Thesis, College of New Rochelle, New Rochelle, NY, 1989.

Preston, Stuart. "Art: A Gallery's Review," ***The New York Times***, January 6, 1962.

Portner, Leslie J. "New Trends—Old Favorites," ***Art News in Washington,*** October 3, 1954.

The Phillips Collection: A Summary Catalogue. Washington, DC: The Phillips Collection, 1985.

Smith, Selma L. ***Printworld Directory of Contemporary Prints and Prices***. Printworld International, Inc., 1982.

Ries, Martin. "Metamorphosis of a Painter," ***Greenwich Village News Magazine***, March-April, 1977, 16-19.

Smithsonian Archive of American Painting, "Richard Kidwell Miller," 1944-1978,Washington, DC.

Wolff, Theodore F. "Why Painting is Worth the Risks," ***The Christian Science Monitor***, June 19, 1990, 12.

Who's Who in America. Chicago: A.N. Marquis, 2002.

Who's Who in American Art. New York: R.R. Bowker, 2001/2002.

Acknowledgements

I wish to extend my sincere gratitude to the following individuals and organizations for their assistance in the preparation of this volume and the accompanying exhibit: The National Society of Arts and Letters, Washington Chapter; the West Virginia Division of Culture and History, Nancy Herhold, Commissioner, and Stephanie Lilly, Curator; the staff of the West Virginia and Regional History Collection, West Virginia University Libraries, including especially Harold Forbes, Frank Tovar, Beth Nardella and Judy Sirk; Dean of West Virginia University Libraries Frances O'Brien; Robert C. Bridges, Curator of Art and Visual Resources, College of Creative Arts, West Virginia University; Sue Crist, Manager, Graphics, West Virginia University Printing Services; Betsy Hughes, Assistant Curator, University of Arizona Museum of Art; James M. and Elizabeth H. Guiher; William Maxwell Davis; Georgiana Morrison; David Alcorn; Deborah Jo Wilson; and above all, Richard and Teresa Miller.

John A. Cuthbert
Curator and Director
West Virginia and Regional History Collection
and Special Collections
West Virginia University Libraries

The National Society of Arts and Letters

Salutes the Lifetime Achievement of

Richard Kidwell Miller

1948 Winner, NSAL Painting Award

Supporting Young Artists Since 1944

Design and layout by John A. Cuthbert using Pagemaker 6.5
Printing by CS Graphics, Singapore